EARTH'S
FINAL HOUR

ED HINDSON

HARVEST HOUSE PUBLISHERS
Eugene, Oregon 97402

Cover by PAZ Design Group, Salem, Oregon

EARTH'S FINAL HOUR
Copyright © 1999 by Ed Hindson
Published by Harvest House Publishers
Eugene, Oregon 97402

Library of Congress Cataloging-in-Publication Data
   Hindson, Edward E.
      Earth's final hour / Ed Hindson.
          p. cm.
        ISBN 1-56507-866-7
        1. Bible—Prophecies—End of the world.   2. End of the world—Biblical teaching.
        I. Title.
      BS649.E63H56   1999
      236'.9—dc21   99-31418
                                               CIP

99 00 01 02 03 04 / BP / 10 9 8 7 6 5 4 3 2 1

To

Dr. Jack Van Impe

*Whose love for Christ's coming
continues to move our hearts
to look for the
Savior's return.*

Acknowledgments

I want to thank several friends and colleagues for their advice and suggestions on this present study. I am especially grateful to Tim LaHaye, Thomas Ice, Randall Price, David Reagan, and Gary Frazier for their helpful insights. I also want to express my gratitude to Mrs. Emily Boothe, who typed the original manuscript.

Contents

The End Is in Sight

Time is running out! The world is speeding on its way to disaster. It is only a matter of time until we approach the final hour of human history. The Bible predicts a conflagration that will engulf the whole world in a war to end all wars. Earth's final hour may be just around the corner.

The Old Testament prophets predicted a day of judgment that they called the "Day of the Lord." Jesus referred to this period as the "great tribulation" (Matthew 24:21 KJV). He warned that unless those days were shortened, no one on earth would survive.

All serious students of biblical prophecy believe that the worst days the world will ever see lie ahead, on the horizon of human history. But the question has always been: *When* will this happen? Throughout the centuries, both serious scholars and wide-eyed fanatics have attempted to determine the time of Christ's coming—without success.

This book is a sincere attempt to help us focus on the things that the Bible clearly predicts about the future. There are several things we can know for certain. But beyond these basic truths, there are many areas where we are left to speculate about *how* these things will eventually be fulfilled. This book is also written as a word of warning and caution against excessive speculation about the future. When we attempt to predict more than God has prophesied, we are in serious trouble.

As we approach the turn of the century—indeed, the turn of the millennium—many people are asking what this may have to do with biblical prophecy. In reality, there are no prophecies about the *timing* of the rapture or the second coming. Nor are there any clear prophecies about the twenty-first century or the third millennium.

We should not be surprised when the new millennium passes and we are all still here. While it is true that Jesus could come at any moment, this does not necessarily mean that He must come on any particular date in order to fulfill biblical prophecy. As we will see, the modern calendar is a man-made device that reflects neither an accurate date for history nor God's ultimate timetable for the world.

In dealing with the problem of excessive speculation about prophetic events, I have pointed to specific issues. In most cases, I have deliberately avoided naming sincere prophecy teachers who themselves have often been guilty of date-setting, date-suggesting or excessive speculations about the last days. It is not my intention to criticize anyone; rather, I want to help all of us be more clear about what the Bible actually says about the future.

I am grateful to all those who love the Lord's appearing and look forward to His coming. I especially want to thank Bob Hawkins Jr., Steve Miller, and the staff at Harvest House for their sincere interest in Bible prophecy. Keep looking up! Your redemption is drawing near (Luke 21:28).

—Ed Hindson
Atlanta, Georgia

The Unfolding Drama of the End Times

The world is changing every day. Things are happening so fast that we can hardly keep up. Every new technological advance hurtles us further into the future. Emerging trends pass us by before we can even comprehend them. The world of tomorrow looks less and less like the world of yesterday with every day that passes. Before we can catch our collective breath, we are hurried on to the next series of events on the horizon of the future.

Many believe we are living in the last days. Earth's final hour could be just around the corner. The next century could well be our last. The dawning of the new millennium may ultimately foreshadow the final sunset on the human race. There are certainly signs of the times that ought to concern us.

Our ever-shifting global community means that the problems of distant lands and peoples become our problems almost instantly. There is little we can do to escape our international and global responsibilities. Crises in Europe, Asia, and the Middle East now impact daily life in America. There is no hiding place on a planet that is interconnected by computer transactions, satellite transmissions, and instantaneous communication. More and more, we are all caught in the tangle of the global web that threatens to engulf us.

Things that once sounded like science fiction are now making headlines in our newspapers: robotic technologies, cyberspace information warfare, electronic surveillance, voice-recognition computer communication, wireless networks and a cashless society. These are the new realities. They no longer refer to things that might someday exist. They already exist.

New technology used to catch people unprepared to deal with it. The telephone was invented in 1876, but it wasn't until 1929 that President Hoover had one installed in the Oval Office at the White House. Today, we can't wait for new technologies to advance. We grab every new gadget that comes along and reorder our lives to accommodate it. The cell phone alone has revolutionized how we work and play. Today's parent can attend a child's ball game and stay in touch with developments at the work office by the mere flick of a switch.

With each new technological advancement comes a growing uneasiness about where all of this is going. We are rushing headlong at a maddening pace without even asking ourselves where we are really headed. The speed of the process has obscured the goal of the journey. We don't know where we are going but we do know that we are in a hurry to get there.

A Date with Destiny

It seems that ours is a generation blinded by the speed of its own journey. We are so busy that we don't want to stop and ask ourselves *where* we are going. And we certainly haven't figured out *why*. We are caught in the rapid-fire pace of the moment and give little thought to the question of what is really happening to us. We are riding the roller coaster of human existence without ever asking where we are going or how we are going to get there.

The Bible predicts several things about the generation of the last days on earth. The prophet Daniel predicted the coming of a "time of distress" unlike anything the world had ever seen (Daniel 12:1). He also described it as a time where "many will go here and there to increase knowledge" (12:4). The Hebrew prophet gives us a glimpse of a world of increased prosperity, travel and education. He foresees a world of advancement and achievement, yet without meaning or purpose. For, despite these great accomplishments, it will still be a society without the answers to its deepest needs.

Jesus also talked about the future as a time when men would "faint from terror, apprehensive of what is coming on the world" (Luke 21:26). The apostle Paul warned, "There will be terrible times in the last days" (2 Timothy 3:1). Peter added, "In the last days scoffers will come … saying, 'Where is this "coming" he promised?'" (2 Peter 3:3-4). Together, they paint a prophetic picture of a time of spiritual blindness, incredible prosperity and impending doom.

During most of the twentieth century there has been a growing awareness that we have been speeding toward a date with destiny. Many believe that time is now running out for planet Earth.[1] Some are surprised we have survived as long as we have. But others claim this is nothing more than "millennial madness."[2] They argue that things are not as bad as they are often depicted. Pointing to failed attempts to set dates for the return of Christ in the past, they quickly debunk the idea that there is little time left before He returns.

As we enter the new millennium, many are asking: How much time is left? Where are we on God's eternal timetable? Can we still believe that Jesus is coming soon? Are the "signs of the times" really occurring today? Are we the terminal generation before the rapture? Can we still believe in the rapture? What will happen when Jesus comes? These are all valid questions that deserve careful and thoughtful answers.

Eschatological Excitement

The closing decade of the twentieth century has been marked by an increased excitement about Bible prophecy ever since Iraq invaded Kuwait in the Persian Gulf War in 1991. Visions of a potential biblical apocalypse spread like wildfire during the early days of the Gulf War only to flicker away quickly when the war ended so suddenly after only four days of ground troop assault. But the coming of the turn of the century and the dawning of the new millennium fanned the flames again.

World news seemed to read like events clearly predicted in biblical prophecies. The European Union (EU) set as its goal the economic and political union of Europe for the first time since the old Roman Empire. Conflicts in the Middle East kept Israel in constant tension with her Arab neighbors. The Middle East in general looked like a powder keg that could blow up at any moment. In the meantime, the United States, on behalf of the Western world, attempted to broker peace in the Middle East with a series of peace treaties between Israel and the Palestinians. Anyone aware of even minimal Bible prophecy could not help see the obvious parallels (see Ezekiel 20:34; Luke 21:20-22; Daniel 2:40-43; 9:25-27).

Ever since the rebirth of the nation of Israel in 1948, there has been a growing awareness among Christians that God's timetable has been moving toward the great climax of biblical prophecy. The miraculous return of the Jews to their biblical homeland after nineteen centuries cannot be dismissed as inconsequential in light of God's sovereign plan for His ancient people. Theoretically, they could be driven out of the land of Israel and return again one day in the future. But this seems highly unlikely in light of the significance of their return after 1,900 years.

We must remember that there were many Bible scholars prior to 1948 who insisted that the Jews would never return to their ancient homeland.[3] Indeed, the rebirth of Israel has not come easily. She has faced resistance continually throughout her first fifty years of existence—1948, 1956, 1967, 1973, and 1991 have all been marked by wars, conflicts and strife on every hand. But Israel has survived, and, indeed, prospered during this time. Today, she is one of the great nations of the world.

Dr. John Walvoord, one of the world's foremost prophetic scholars, has said: "Never before in history have all the factors been present for the fulfillment of prophecy relating to end-time religious trends and events. Only in our generation have the combined revival of Israel, the formation of a world church, the increasing power of Islam, the rise of the occult, and the worldwide spread of atheistic philosophy all been present as a dramatic setting for the final fulfillment of prophecy. The road to Armageddon is always well prepared."[4]

Dr. Randall Price adds: "If we believe that God is active in the affairs of His world, directing people and events according to His plan, then we should be looking at the *people* (Jewish People) and the *place* (Land of Israel) where the fulfillment of these things will occur."[5] Price reminds us that the major prophecies of future events relate to the nation and people of Israel. In contrast, there are only a handful of prophecies about the future of the church. The Bible predicts the growth of the church (Matthew 16:18); the worldwide proclamation of the gospel (Matthew 24:14); and the eventual rapture of the church to heaven (John 14:3; 1 Thessalonians 4:16-17; 1 Corinthians 15:51-52).

Keeping Our Focus Clear

The major focus of biblical prophecy concerns the nation and people of Israel. Prophetic passages dealing with the tribulation period (Matthew 24:22), the rise of the antichrist (2 Thessalonians 2:3-8), the signing of a peace treaty (Daniel 9:25-27), the invasion of Israel by Gentile forces (Zechariah 14:12-13), and the battle of Armageddon (Revelation 16:16) all focus on the nation of Israel and its significant place in the great end-times drama.[6] This important factor cannot be overlooked in the study of Bible prophecy. Those who miss this point will miss the real significance of what God is doing to prepare the stage of world events for the end times.

Keeping our focus on Israel will also keep us from getting sidetracked by world events that have *no direct* prophetic significance. While many world events contribute to the general stage-setting for the last days, they are often merely ancillary events in light of the general prophetic picture in Scripture. This means that incidents like Iraq's invasion of Kuwait or crises in the Balkans may be a part of God's great plan moving us closer to the specific fulfillment of biblical prophecies, but these incidents are not clearly prophesied in Scripture. There are no specific prophecies about Saddam Hussein, Boris Yeltsin or Slobodon Milosevic anywhere in the Bible.

Students of Bible prophecy need to keep these distinctions clearly in mind as they approach the Scriptures. We may interpret current events in light of biblical prophecy, but we dare not interpret biblical prophecy in light of current events. Randall Price observes: "This 'common sense' principle is a necessary corrective to discourage what has been called 'newspaper exegesis,' or interpreting the biblical prophecies based on stories that appear in the media."[7]

Price provides the following guidelines for a proper interpretation of biblical prophecies:

1. Interpret current events in light of the Bible, not the Bible in light of current events.

2. Fulfillment of most prophetic events related to Israel will not take place until after the rapture.

3. Does the biblical text provide enough data to draw a correspondence with current events?

4. Distinguish between the last days of the church and the last days of Israel.[8]

Vague *general* parallels do not constitute *specific* prophetic fulfillment. Most end-times prophecies focus on broad, general themes: increase of wickedness (Matthew 24:12); rise of false prophets (Matthew 24:4,24); the return of Israel to the land (Ezekiel 20:34; 37:12-21); the development of a global economy (Revelation 13:16-17); the formation of a world government (Revelation 13:8; 17:15-18); and a false sense of peace and security (1 Thessalonians 5:2-3). There is nothing in these general prophecies that specifically refers to such things as computers, satellite technology, credit cards, implanted chips, Y2K, the World Wide Web, the United Nations, NATO, UFOs or New Age religions.

These things may or may not be related to biblical prophecies. Time will be the judge of which of these had anything to do with the ultimate fulfillment of future events. If we know what the Bible is predicting in general, then we can examine specific *possibilities* in light of how they might relate to the eventual fulfillment of prophecy. Beyond that, we dare not say that we know how these various current events will eventually unfold into specific prophetic fulfillment.

Why the Need for Caution?

Overstatement and excessive speculation about Bible prophecy have given critics of prophecy ample ammunition to reject prophetic fulfillment altogether. This tactic is used constantly by *preterists* who believe that most prophecies were already fulfilled in the past with the Roman army's destruction of Jerusalem in A.D. 70. Beyond that, they see little future prophecy in the Bible except for the ultimate triumph of Christ. In their discussions of *pretribulationalists,* who believe in a literal future fulfillment, their focus is almost always to point out wild and ridiculous speculations that have failed to come true and thereby imply that all *futurists* are guilty of such excesses.[9]

Favorite examples of misguided prophetic speculations include:

- William Miller and the Adventists predicted the return of Christ in 1843 (later "revised" to 1844).

- Charles Russell, founder of the Jehovah's Witnesses, predicted the return of Christ in 1914 to establish His Kingdom on earth.

- Herbert W. Armstrong, then leader of the Worldwide Church of God, predicted the second coming of Christ in 1972.

- Charles Taylor has "suggested" eleven dates for the rapture from 1975 to 1989.

- Edgar Whisenant wrote *88 Reasons Why the Rapture Will Be in 1988* (later revised *ad infinitum, ad nauseum*)!

- Elizabeth Clare Prophet, New Age leader of the Church Universal and Triumphant, predicted the Battle of Armageddon in 1990.

- Mary Stewart Relfe, a self-proclaimed "New Testament prophet," indicated she believed Christ would return before 1990.

- Lee Jang Rim of South Korea's Dami Missionary Church predicted the rapture on October 28, 1992.

- Harold Camping, American radio pastor, predicted the rapture would occur in 1994.

- Others suggest the year 2000 is "a probable terminal date for the 'last days.'"[10]

Evangelical historian Mark Noll has warned: "The verdict of history seems clear. Great spiritual gain comes from living under the expectation of Christ's return. But wisdom and restraint are also in order. At the very least, it would be well for those in our age who predict details and dates for the End to remember how many before them have misread the signs of the times."[11]

The attempts at date-setting, or even date-suggesting, have all run contrary to the fact that the Bible itself sets no date for the rapture of the church! Even well-meaning "suggestions" must be viewed as misguided speculations. In the end, they confuse sincere believers and provide fodder for the critics of genuine biblical prophecy. Their favorite tactic is to list all the suggested dates for the rapture or candidates for the antichrist (e.g., Adolf Hitler, John Kennedy, Henry Kissinger, Mikhail Gorbachev, Prince Charles), and then debunk all pretribulationist futurists as fanatics.

Critics of biblical prophecy rarely refer to the fact that pre-tribulational scholars like John Walvoord, Charles Ryrie, Charles Dyer, Dwight Pentecost, Thomas Ice, Randall Price, and Harold Wilmington, or popularizers like Tim LaHaye, David Jeremiah, Ed Dobson, Jerry Falwell and John Hagee have *never* set any dates for the rapture or the second coming of Christ. Serious students of prophecy have the same disdain for prophetic misrepresentations that critics of prophecy have. Richard Kyle observes that prophetic speculators are rarely trained theologians. He states, "Modern prophecy has often been done by amateurs. Some have training in science or engineering, but few in theology or history. Despite their disdain for traditional higher education, these popularizers are eager for intellectual respectability.... Despite deriding academia, they often fashion themselves as educated people—sometimes with honorary or bogus doctorates."[12]

B.J. Oropeza of the Christian Research Institute in Irvine, California, gives three important reasons to avoid date-suggesting. He writes: "Some respected evangelicals suggest dates without dogmatically affirming a particular date for the end."[13] The problem with this approach is that it often implies date-setting in the mind of the reader or listener. Oropeza lists these important cautions:

1. *Date-suggesting encourages others to set dates.* It also lends credibility to their arguments. If a well-known Christian leader "suggests" a possible date for the return of Christ, a less responsible person may quote him as the authority for the date they have dogmatically set.

2. *Date-suggesting flirts with being disobedient to Scripture.* Since the Bible clearly tells us that no one knows the date, is it not contrary to Scripture to even suggest a date?

3. *Many people do not distinguish between date-suggesting and date-setting.* Some people naïvely assume that the suggested date is actually a fact of Bible prophecy. When it doesn't come true, they often become disillusioned and reject biblical prophecy altogether.

The greatest danger of uncontrolled and excessive prophetic speculation is that it almost always leads to an overreaction against legitimate prophetic study and interpretation. This is especially true when the speculation arises from someone who also happens to believe in the rapture. They immediately become an example of why we shouldn't believe in the rapture at all.

Just a Coincidence?

Another line of argumentation used by critics of biblical prophecy is that the events of the twentieth century just *coincidentally* appeared to follow the pretribulational view of prophecy. During the early years of the twentieth century, the world stood on the brink of war. In 1913, R.A. Torrey said: "All our present peace plans will end in the most awful wars and conflicts this old world ever saw."[14]

Richard Kyle observes: "The years after 1914 gave premillennialism a tremendous boost.... The basic prophecies of the early dispensationalists in the nineteenth century began to take concrete form in the early twentieth century.... The apparent fulfillment of ancient biblical prophecies enabled dispensationalism to take solid root in the evangelical subculture."[15]

Indeed, the list of historical and prophetic coincidences was amazing:

- The Balfour Declaration called for the return of the Jews to Palestine in 1917.

- British forces under General Edmund Allenby captured Jerusalem from the Turks in 1917.

- The Turkish Empire lost control of the Middle East to the British in 1918 after World War I.

- The formation of the League of Nations in 1919 pointed to the potential of World government after World War I.

- Great Britain established a protectorate over Palestine from 1920 to 1948, allowing more Jews to return to their homeland.

- Hitler's persecution of the Jewish people during the holocaust of World War II forced thousands of European Jews to flee to Palestine.

- The formation of the United Nations revived concerns about a world government.

- In May 1948, the UN declared Israel a sovereign state.

- Israel has survived as a nation while having to constantly defend herself against the aggression of various Arab states (Egypt, Jordan, Syria, Iraq). Today, Israel is a prosperous and flourishing nation with a strong military presence in the Middle East.

- Economic prosperity and advanced technology have created a global economy tied together by computer transfers and satellite transmissions.

- Western powers, led by the United States, have continually encouraged peace in the Middle East by urging peace treaties between Israel and the various Arab factions.

Kyle states: "The turn of world events played an even greater role in solidifying the credibility of dispensational eschatology."[16] Almost every critic of dispensationalism acknowledges this fact and promptly *dismisses* it as though it were irrelevant! Perhaps it is time for these critics to own up to the fact that the dispensational view of the future comes closer to reality than any other eschatological view. Indeed, recently Richard Mouw, president of Fuller Theological Seminary, admitted that the modern world is a "vindication for the dispensationalist's view of history." Mouw asks, "Who had a better sense of what was going to happen in the twentieth century? It seems obvious that Protestant liberalism was simply wrong in its predictions, whereas much of the dispensationalist scenario was vindicated."[17]

The *general picture* of the future is clearly stated in biblical prophecy. What is not always clear is how the specific pieces of the prophetic puzzle will actually come together in the end. Since the Bible sets no dates or time limits on the fulfillment of prophecy, we are all left guessing how close we are to the end.

This is a very important truth to remember when attempting to interpret any prophetic passage. Given our present perspective, it may seem that certain current events will imminently fulfill certain prophetic predictions. But as time moves on, those assumptions may prove premature.

There are also events that "pop up" out of nowhere that are nothing more than small pieces of the general prophetic picture. These events are rarely foreseen by prophetic writers. Nobody predicted Iraq's invasion of Kuwait in 1991 or the resulting Gulf War in 1992. Neither did anyone predict the military crisis between NATO and the Yugoslavian Serbs in 1999. The reason is simple: These events are *not* predicted in the Bible! The closest possible parallel one can draw is simply to relate them to the larger themes of biblical prophecy, like war in the Middle East or the unification of Europe in the last days. Even then, this correspondence usually can only be seen *after* the fact and not before.

How Close Is the End?

The questions most frequently asked any prophecy teacher are: How close is the end? How much time is left? So, when do you think Jesus is coming? Unfortunately, the greatest danger for prophecy teachers is the temptation to answer such questions. Even a casual opinion, cautiously expressed, can give the impression that you really believe the end is just around the corner. Therefore, we must always remind ourselves that we really don't know how much time is left on God's timetable.

There are certain events predicted in biblical prophecy that appear to be in the process of being fulfilled today. But there are other events that still appear to be a long way from their final fulfillment. How do we reconcile these with a belief in the imminent return of Christ to rapture the church? Let me suggest several considerations:

1. *There is no predicted event that must be fulfilled before the rapture takes place.* Jesus could come at any time to call His bride home to heaven. Our Lord's commands to "keep watching" and "be ready" (Matthew 24:42-44) still apply.

2. *There are, however, certain events that may yet unfold before the rapture.* There is no biblical limitation on such possibilities as nuclear war, international terrorism, isolated wars in Europe or the Middle East, or the rebuilding of the Jewish Temple. These may not happen prior to the rapture, but we cannot exclude that possibility on the basis of Scripture alone.

3. *As time marches on, the prophetic picture continues to become more clear.* We can only look ahead from our current perspective. But already we can see that some things that still seemed vague twenty or thirty years ago are now clearer, such as the development of a global economy.

4. *We cannot project the future based on current events alone.* Our only clear guide to the future is biblical truth. Everything else is little more than an "educated guess." World leaders will come and go. Soon there will be a whole new set of players giving rise to new speculations about their possible roles in the end-times drama.

5. *The Bible itself is the only clear guide to understanding the future.* God has given us "great and precious promises" and the "word of the prophets" to give us a certainty about the future (2 Peter 1:4,19). True biblical prophecies are not of human origin or private interpretation. They are truths expressed by the Holy Spirit, who moved divinely inspired writers to predict the future as God sees it.

What We Can Expect

Speculating about the future beyond what the Bible itself predicts is a dangerous game. Psychics make hundreds of predictions every year that never come true. But a gullible general public doesn't seem to care. People quickly run out to buy the list of predictions for next year. Bible prophecy, however, does not work that way. The prophets sent by God made many predictions thousands of years ago about the first and second comings of Christ. Their prophecies have stood the test of time; many have been fulfilled and there are more prophecies about certain future events that are inevitable:

- The spread of the gospel and the ***growth of the church*** through the worldwide evangelism of all nations (Matthew 24:14)

- The rise of ***religious apostasy*** in the last days, leading to widespread sin and lawlessness (2 Thessalonians 2:3)

- The ***rapture of the church*** (true believers) to heaven prior to the great tribulation judgments (Revelation 3:10)

- The ***rise of the antichrist*** and the ***false prophet*** to control the "new world order" of the end times (Revelation 13:1-4; 11-18)

- The ***tribulation period*** on the earth with widespread ecological destruction, war, and famine (Matthew 24:21-22)

- The ***triumphal return of Christ*** with His church to overthrow the antichrist and bind Satan for 1,000 years (Revelation 19:11-16; 20:1-2)

- The ***millennial kingdom*** of Christ on earth for 1,000 years of peace and prosperity (Revelation 20:4-6)

Beyond these key events, we can only speculate about what will happen. The Bible seems to predict an age of unparalleled selfism in the last days (2 Timothy 3:1-6). It seems to indicate an age of skepticism and unbelief—a time when people will scoff at the idea of Christ's return (2 Peter 3:3-4). It also appears that this age will be marked by global wealth and prosperity (Revelation 18:11-19).

The next generation could well be the last one on earth. Social issues like poverty, prejudice, and racial hatred continue to plague our world. The riots in our nation's cities only serve to underscore the depth of racial tension in our own country. In the meantime, racial, ethnic, and religious conflicts threaten to tear apart Eastern Europe and the Commonwealth of Independent States that made up the former Soviet Union. All indications are that the years ahead will be marked by the widespread production of nuclear bombs by developing nations, some of which are led by trigger-happy, egotistical military dictators. And all of this is taking place in the midst of continued deterioration of the earth's atmosphere and environment.

The only real hope for planet Earth is the return of Christ. Ecologists, naturalists, and conservationists will never save this planet. New Age politicians with global aspirations will not save this globe. Antinuclear demonstrators will not save the earth. The Bible tells us that "the creation waits in eager expectation for the sons of God to be revealed" when Jesus Christ returns (Romans 8:19).

When Jesus returns with His raptured church, the deterioration of the planet will cease. The devastation that resulted from the war of the tribulation period will be reversed. The earth will blossom under the peaceful rule of the Prince of peace. But without Christ on the throne, this planet is headed for serious trouble. Only He can overrule the degradation of sin, the destruction of war, and the devastation of the planet.

Are We Running Out of Time?

Many people believe we are living in the end times. They are convinced that the world is a powder keg waiting to explode at any minute. They foresee the world being plunged into a series of cataclysmic wars that will bring the human race to the precipice of extinction. By the time these apocalyptic wars end, perhaps as much as three-fourths of the earth's population will be destroyed.

No right-thinking person wants war, no matter what his view of the end times. We all sense the ominous finality of the biblical predictions about the end and pray that God will stay His hand of judgment on our world. But only a fool could think that human beings are clever enough to avoid a final confrontation of disastrous consequences. We may dodge the apocalyptic bullet a few more times, but sooner or later, we will have to face the final moment of history.

Such concerns are not new. The biblical record has stood complete for nearly 2,000 years. Its prophecies of future events may dazzle us and baffle us at the same time. Commenting on the final consummation of the world many years ago, Tertullian, an early church leader, said: "We pray for the postponement of the end."[1] By contrast, the apostle Peter wrote that we should "look forward to the day of God and speed its coming" (2 Peter 3:12). Thus, Christians have often found themselves caught between their present realities and their future expectations.

We are not afraid of the future because we have read the "last chapter" of the book and we know how it all turns out. At the same time, most of us are in no hurry to rush the process. We have lives to live, responsibilities to meet and schedules to keep. But as we rush about our daily routines we have a growing uneasiness that much of what we are doing is all in vain in light of eternity.

The Bible reminds us that eventually, "the day of the Lord will come like a thief. The heavens will disappear with a roar; the elements will be destroyed by fire, and the earth and everything in it will be laid bare" (2 Peter 3:10). In the light of eternity, everything earthly is temporary except the eternal souls of men and women. God is far more concerned about what is going to happen to *you* than about what is going to happen to the earth.

Christians have long been interested in biblical prophecies of the end of the world. St. Augustine said, "The following events shall come to pass: Elijah shall come; the Jews shall believe; the Antichrist shall persecute; Christ will judge; the dead shall rise; the good and the wicked shall be separated; the world shall be burned and renewed. All these things we believe shall come to pass; but how, or in what order, human understanding cannot perfectly teach us, but only the experience of the events themselves."[2] Augustine's advice is well stated. Only when the events are actually fulfilled will their culmination become obvious.

Looking Ahead

In the meantime, the Bible is full of unfulfilled prophecies that point to some future fulfillment. These include:

1. The rapture of the church (1 Thessalonians 4:13-18).

2. The revival of the Roman Empire (Daniel 7:7, 24).

3. The rise of the antichrist (Revelation 13:1-18).

4. The apostate world church (Revelation 17:1-15).

5. A seven-year peace treaty with Israel (Daniel 9:25-27).

6. The peace treaty with Israel broken (Daniel 7:23; 9:25-27).

7. Martyrdom of those who refuse to worship the beast (Revelation 13:1-15).

8. Divine judgments: seals, trumpets, bowls (Revelation 6–18).

9. A world war culminating in the battle of Armageddon (Revelation 16:12-16).

10. The triumphal return of Christ (Revelation 19:11-21).

11. The millennial kingdom (Revelation 20:1-6).

12. The great white throne judgment (Revelation 20:11-15).

13. Eternity: new heavens and a new earth (Revelation 21:1-2).

David Reagan points out that there are dozens of passages that refer to the future reign of Christ on earth.[3] These include:

- Psalm 2:6-9. The Messiah will reign over "the ends of the earth" from Mount Zion.

- Psalm 22:27-31. The Messiah will rule "over the nations."

- Psalm 110. The Lord will make the Messiah's enemies His "footstool" and He shall rule over His enemies.

- Isaiah 9:6-7. The Messiah will rule from "David's throne" in Jerusalem.

- Isaiah 24:21-23. The Messiah will "reign on Mount Zion and in Jerusalem."

- Jeremiah 23:5. The Lord will raise up "a righteous Branch" from the line of David to reign over Israel.

- Ezekiel 37:24-28. Referring to the Messiah, the prophet says, "David my servant will be their prince forever."

- Daniel 7:13-18. The Messiah ("Son of Man") is given dominion over all the kingdoms of earth by God the Father ("Ancient of Days").

- Micah 4:1-7. "The Lord will rule over them in Mount Zion."

- Zechariah 14:1-9. The Messiah will return to the Mount of Olives and "the Lord will be King over the whole earth."

- Luke 1:26-38. The angel Gabriel promised Mary that her son would be given the "throne of His father David" and that He would "reign over the house of Jacob forever."

- Revelation 19:15-16. Jesus will return as "King of kings and Lord of lords," and He will rule the nations.

Each of these prophecies reminds us that there will be a literal future reign of Christ on earth that fulfills these glorious promises. David Larsen summarizes these promises, saying, "The whole bulk of Old Testament prophecy points to the establishment of a Kingdom of peace on the earth when the law will go forth from Mount Zion."[4] Thomas Ice and Timothy Demy observe: "Even though the Bible speaks descriptively throughout

about the millennial kingdom, it was not until the final book—
Revelation—that the length of His Kingdom is revealed."[5]

John Walvoord notes that the English word *millennium* comes
from the Latin word *mille,* meaning "thousand." The Greek word
for thousand is *chilias* and is used six times in Revelation 20 to
express the duration of Christ's kingdom on earth.[6] The millennial kingdom of one thousand years follows the tribulation period
and precedes eternity. From the divine perspective, there is still a
great deal of time left for planet Earth. Both the tribulation
period and the millennium are yet to come.

The real question about how much time is left refers to the
time remaining before the rapture of the church. If we are really
running out of time, then we ought to be able to pinpoint certain
prophecies that indicate the time may be short.

Signs of the Times

Jesus said: "There will be signs in the sun, moon and stars. On
earth, nations will be in anguish ... for the heavenly bodies will be
shaken" (Luke 21:25-26). Then He added: "When these things
begin to take place, stand up and lift up your heads, because your
redemption is drawing near" (Luke 21:28). Our Lord clearly indicated that certain "signs" would precede His return. He also said
"that day will close on you unexpectedly." Therefore, He urged us,
"Be always on the watch, and pray that you may be able to escape
all that is about to happen" (Luke 21:34-36).

It has often been noted that there are no signs for the rapture
of the church. It is an imminent event that could take place at
any time. The "signs" mentioned in the Bible refer to the return
of Christ. But if such signs warn us that the return is near, they
also serve to warn that the rapture is even nearer. If we see
Christmas decorations in the mall in October, we not only know
that Christmas is coming but that Thanksgiving is coming even
sooner. So it is with the signs of the times.

David Reagan notes: "There are over 300 prophecies in the Hebrew Scriptures about the first coming of the Messiah. But many are repetitions. When you cull out all the repetitious prophecies, you are left with a total of 109 which were fulfilled in the life of Jesus."[7] When the Pharisees and Sadducees asked Jesus to prove that He was the Messiah, He told them that they had failed to read the "signs of the times" (Matthew 16:1-14). Reagan argues that if signs of the first coming were literally fulfilled, then we have every reason to believe the signs of the second coming will be literally fulfilled as well.

Reagan provides the best overview of the "signs" of the second coming that I have ever seen. He divides them into *seven categories:*[8]

1. ***Signs of Nature*** (see Matthew 24:7; Mark 13:8; Luke 21:11)

   Famine
   Earthquakes
   Plagues
   Unusual weather

2. ***Signs of Society*** (Matthew 24:37-39; 2 Timothy 3:1-4)

   Lawlessness
   Violence
   Immorality
   Greed
   Selfishness
   Hedonism
   Rebellion
   Despair

3. ***Spiritual Signs*** (Matthew 24:5-11; 2 Thessalonians 2:3; 2 Timothy 4:1-14)

   Negative
       False christs and false prophets
       Apostasy in the professing church
       Widespread heresies

    Movement toward one world religion
    Persecution of true believers
    Outbreak of demonic activity
   Positive (Matthew 24:14; Joel 2:28-29; Amos 9:11)
    Outpouring of the Holy Spirit
    Revival of Davidic worship
    Worldwide evangelism
    Understanding of Bible prophecy

4. *Political Signs* (Ezekiel 37:1-12; Zechariah 12:1-14; Matthew 24:6-7; Revelation 16–18)

 Regathering of Israel
 Arab hostility toward Israel
 Wars and rumors of wars
 Reunification of Europe
 Movement toward a global economy
 Movement toward a world government

5. *Technological Signs* (Revelation 6–8; 11:3-12; 13:14-18; Daniel 12:4)

 Nuclear weapons
 Television and satellite transmission
 Robotics
 Computer and laser technology
 High-speed transportation

6. *Accelerator Signs* (Revelation 9:15-16; Daniel 12:4; Matthew 24:8-12; 2 Timothy 3:1-4)

 Population explosion
 Increase in knowledge
 Increase in violence
 Increase in transportation
 Rapid disintegration of society
 "Birth pains," increasing in frequency and intensity

7. *Signs of Israel* (Ezekiel 37:1-12; Zechariah 12:1-6; Zephaniah 3:9)

 Regathering of the Jewish people

Reestablishment of the state of Israel
Reclamation of the land of Israel
Revival of the Hebrew language
Resurgence of the military
Refocusing of world politics
Reoccupation of Jerusalem

The amazing thing about these "signs of the times" is that most of them are in place today. We are not standing at some point in history where such things seem incredible and beyond our comprehension. To the contrary, this list of "signs" sounds like our daily newspapers. We read about and hear about such events almost daily. Consider just the *basic signs:*

1. Israel is back in the land as a sovereign state.

2. There is constant conflict in the Middle East.

3. Weapons of mass destruction already exist.

4. European nations are forming the European Union.

5. Western powers are attempting to guarantee Israel's peace and security.

6. We already have a global economy.

7. The potential of a world government is already in place.

One would have to be blind to current events to miss the fact that these all parallel specific biblical prophecies about the last days. Taken collectively, their impact is even more dramatic. The fact that all seven of these basic "signs" are already in place ought to indicate that we are well down the road to the final fulfillment of the prophecies of the end times.

The existence of these factors, in and of themselves, does not necessarily mean that these are the final forms of the biblical predictions. But they are certainly very close to it. Israel could be removed from the Promised Land and return again in the future.

But it doesn't seem logical that the Jews would return prematurely unless it were in fulfillment of the prophetic promises to Israel. Nuclear weapons may not be the final form of the weapons of mass destruction described in Revelation 6–18, but what could be any worse? Current attempts at the European Union could fail, but the immediate proximity of the modern world by telephones, computers, satellites, and rapid transportation couldn't bring it much closer together than it is already.

Could There Be Any Delays?

Jesus Himself indicated that He would be gone "a long time" (Matthew 25:19). However, He gave no indication of how much time would pass until He returned. In fact, He deliberately left the impression that He could return at any time, even when least expected (Matthew 24:50). The basic timing passages in the New Testament suggest the *following sequence:*

1. No one knows the time of His coming (Matthew 24:36).

2. We are to evangelize the whole world until He returns (Matthew 24:14; 28:18-20).

3. He will be gone "a long time" (Matthew 25:19).

4. Unbelievers will scoff at the idea of His return (2 Peter 3:3-34).

5. Believers are to "watch" and "be ready" for Him to come at any moment (Matthew 24:42-44).

6. He will return when least expected (Matthew 24:50).

7. He will come suddenly (Revelation 22:7,12).

The only other significant biblical passages referring to the timing of Jesus' coming have to do with the "end of the age" (Matthew 24:3). Our Lord reminds us that the coming of wars, famines, and earthquakes are "the beginning of birth pains," but they themselves do not mean that "the end" has come (Matthew 24:6-8). In other words, just because the end is near doesn't mean the end is here! Jesus said "the end" would not come until the "gospel of the kingdom" was preached "in the whole world as a testimony to all nations" (Matthew 24:14). This same idea is emphasized in the Great Commission when Jesus commanded His disciples to "go and make disciples of all nations" and promised to be with them to the "end of the age" (Matthew 28:19-20).

People sometimes use the phrase "if the Lord tarries," referring to the length of time before He returns. However, the Bible says: "He who is coming will come and will not delay" (Hebrews 10:37, which quotes Habakkuk 2:3). The context implies that even if the fulfillment of the prophecy seems to be delayed, wait patiently because the One who is coming will not be delayed but will come on time.

Peter makes a similar reference to the patience of God in dealing with us (2 Peter 3:8-15). God is patient, not wanting any to perish, but His patience cannot be viewed as a delay of action on His part. In fact, Peter tells us to live "holy and godly lives" in view of His coming "as you look forward to the day of God and speed its coming" (3:11-12). This raises the question of whether the time of the end is fluid or fixed. Jesus said, "If those days had not been cut short, no one would survive, but for the sake of the elect those days will be shortened" (Matthew 24:22).

At the same time, Jesus said, "No one knows about that day or hour...but only the Father" (Matthew 24:36). Here our Lord indicates that the time is fixed by the sovereign will and purpose of God the Father. Much has been debated about this in Christian circles. Some believe the exact time is fixed and others believe we can speed up that time by increasing our effort to evangelize the world.

Jesus also referred to the days ahead as the "times of the Gentiles" (Luke 21:24). Stanley Ellisen says, "The 'times of the Gentiles' is that period of time in which the Gentiles have dominion over Israel, especially Jerusalem.... Therefore, this period began when Jerusalem was captured by Nebuchadnezzar in 605 B.C., and will be completed when Christ comes to set up His everlasting Kingdom on earth."[9] By this reckoning, Israel is still under the "times of the Gentiles" today. The Church Age is part of that time period but is not synonymous with it. The "times of the Gentiles" will continue beyond the rapture of the church and include the antichrist's role in relation to Israel during the tribulation period.

From a biblical standpoint, several things are clear about the timing of God's prophecies:

1. Jesus has already been gone "a long time."

2. Israel is already back in her ancient land.

3. The world scene looks a great deal like the one pictured in Bible prophecy.

All outward indications seem to point to the fact that the time may be very short until Jesus comes. Most of the biblical prophecies of the end times have either been fulfilled *already*, or are in the process of being fulfilled at the *present* or could easily be fulfilled in the immediate *future*. There are no major prophetic events that could prohibit the rapture from taking place at any moment.

Time Marches On

As time marches on, the prophetic picture of the future continues to become clearer and more focused. While it is true that Jesus could come at any moment, every day that passes gives us a clearer picture of what is coming in the future. There may well be several new developments in the next century that clarify the prophetic picture even more. There is nothing in the Bible that specifically refers to the twenty-first century or the third millennium of the Christian era.

There is an old nonbiblical Jewish legend, the so-called "Prophecy of Elijah" that claimed the world would last only 6,000 years.[10] In time, some Christians adopted this scheme to suggest the following time sequence:

Old Testament era	4,000 years
New Testament era	2,000 years
Millennial Kingdom	1,000 years
Total	7,000 years

This schematic is generally supported by quoting 2 Peter 3:8, "With the Lord a day is like a thousand years, and a thousand years are like a day." The seven thousand years are then paralleled to the seven days of creation for further validity. The seventh day (Sabbath) is compared to the seventh millennium as a period of divine rest.

There are several problems with this whole idea. *First,* we already have run out of time! More than 2,000 years of the Christian era have already passed. If our current calendar is off, as most believe, then we have already seen more than 2,000 years pass since the birth of Christ.

The present calendar was devised by Pope Gregory the Great in the sixteenth century, based on an earlier calendar of Dionysius the Short, commissioned by Pope John I in A.D. 525. The problem is that both calendars have apparently set the wrong date for the birth of Christ, which almost all biblical scholars now set at 4 B.C. based on the death of Herod the Great in that year. If the wise men visited Herod before his death, then Jesus would have to have been born sometime between 6 and 4 B.C. If the calendar is off by at least four years, then 1996 was the year 2000 since the birth of Christ (*Anno Domini,* "the year of our Lord"). To complicate matters further, the year 2000 is the year 5760 on the Jewish calendar—240 years short of the 6,000-year total.[11]

Second, there is no reason to take Peter's statement about the longevity of God's grace to have anything to do with a specific time frame by which to predict the future. *Third,* the millennium is a time of great activity, not a sabbath of rest. While the 6,000-year theory is clever and interesting, it must be recognized for what it is—a Jewish myth!

There is nothing in the Bible that indicates that there will only be 2,000 years of church history or that Jesus must return in or near A.D. 2000. As we move further and further beyond the year 2000, this will become more and more obvious. Those who insist on hanging their dispensationalism on this date will only provide ammunition for the critics of dispensational theology to blast away at its foundational truths.

The older we become, the more we realize how *quickly* time passes. When you are in your twenties, ten years seems like a long time. By the time you reach your sixties, ten years won't seem that long anymore. Time is marching on every single day, and we cannot do anything to slow it down. But we can be sure that every day that passes brings us that much closer to the end. One day the trumpet will sound and the church will go home to glory. In the meantime, we cannot get sidetracked by date-setters, prophetic speculators or even well-intended predictions of the future. Only God knows exactly what lies ahead and how much time is left.

What Can We Expect?

There are some things prophesied in Scripture that have not yet come to pass. Therefore, we can expect that these will continue to be formulated in the years ahead. While Christ could come at any moment, if He does not come soon, we should expect to see these developments begin to occur. I can only *speculate* on how these things might develop in light of general prophetic truth. Beyond that, none of us dare say more than the Bible itself says on these matters.

Certain events already seem to be in place—the nation of Israel, the consolidation of the Western powers, tension in the Middle East, the global economy and the move toward a world government. At the same time, there are several things predicted in Scripture that do *not* exist at this time:

1. *Israel has not regained its original biblical borders.*

The rebirth of the state of Israel in 1948 is indeed a miracle of God. However, that was only the beginning of the fulfillment of God's promise to restore Israel to her former greatness. In 1967 and 1973, Israel added further territory, including the entire city of Jerusalem. But there are still continued disputes over the Golan Heights, the West Bank and even such biblical sites as Jericho and Bethlehem. Beyond this is the fact that David's kingdom included much of what today exists in Jordan and Syria (2 Samuel 8). Will Israel capture more territory in the days ahead or will territory be given to her as a part of a peace settlement? Will the biblical borders be realized before the millennium? Only time will tell.

2. *The rebuilding of the temple has not begun.*

The fact that Paul indicates that the antichrist will sit "in God's temple, proclaiming himself to be God" (2 Thessalonians 2:4), indicates that the Jews will eventually rebuild the Temple (Third Temple) in Jerusalem. Today, the Temple Mount is occupied by the Islamic shrine called the Dome of the Rock. Jews are not allowed to sacrifice on the Temple Mount. While many pious Jews are praying for and even preparing instruments of worship for the Third Temple, there is no temple under construction at this time. Misguided attempts by fanatical rabbis to lay the foundation stone of the temple do not represent official Israeli government policy. Arguments about the exact location of the Holy of Holies notwithstanding, there can be no Jewish Temple on the Temple Mount as long as the Muslims hold control. What does this mean for the future? Will the Dome of the Rock be destroyed? Will the Muslims lose control of the Temple Mount? Will a new Temple be built before the rapture? Will the antichrist authorize the building of the Temple? Only time will tell.[12]

3. *We do not yet have a world government.*

The current international situation revolves around the relationship of the United States of America to the United Nations. While there is no world government at this time, all the elements of such an international body are already in place. International sanctions are approved through the Security Council of the U.N., including military action against rogue states, that defy international consensus. The World Court and other international bodies function in relation to the sovereign states of the world community. Several questions remain unanswered. How long will it take for a world government to form? How will individual nations relinquish their own sovereignty? What will happen to the Muslim world and its relationship to the international community? What role will Russia play in the future? Only time will tell.

4. *There is no world religion at this time.*

The Bible indicates there will be a world religion in the future dominated by the false prophet. But there is no world religion at the present time. Indeed, there is no consensus among Christians, let alone among Muslims, Jews, Hindus, Buddhists, New Age adherents, or Satanists. It is true that philosophical relativism tends to make a religion out of religious tolerance, but that doesn't mean tolerance is the final form of apostate religion. New Age influences are strong, but there is no real proof that this is the religion of the last days. It may well be that the final form of the world religion will not appear until after the rapture of the church. Many questions still remain unanswered at this time. Will the world religion unify all religions or is it an apostate form of Christianity? Will the antichrist oppose Christianity or attempt to imitate it in some way? Only time will tell.

5. *The antichrist is not on the scene at this moment.*

It is certainly possible that the person who will become the antichrist is already alive. But his identity cannot be revealed until after the rapture when the church is removed and its restraining influence is gone (2 Thessalonians 2:7-12). Since Jesus said that no one, including the angels, knows the time of His coming (Matthew 24:36), we must conclude that even Satan does not know when the rapture will occur. He, too, is a created and finite being and does not know the mind of God. Therefore, Satan's hands are tied until God makes the ultimate move. Satan can select potential candidates for the antichrist, but he cannot move the antichrist on the scene until God gives the sign. Satan, in the meantime, is left waiting for the sound of the trumpet just like us.[13] Is the antichrist alive and well? Is he moving into power at this time? Can he be identified? Only time will tell.

The Road Ahead

The *main features* of Bible prophecy are clearly stated in Scripture. From these, we can draw some general conclusions about what to expect on the road ahead. Beyond these, the *details* of future prophetic events are deliberately obscure until their final fulfillment. Therefore, we need to be careful not to make too many assumptions based on our limited perspective at our moment in time. It may be that as time passes, the details will become clearer to us.

The greatest error made by prophetic speculators is attempting to read the *future* through the eyes of the *present*. At this moment in time, a certain situation may appear to be the fulfillment of some prophetic truth (e.g., implanted computer chips are the "mark" of the beast). Later, it may become clear that the Bible was referring to something else altogether. We cannot run ahead of God's timetable. He knows exactly what He is doing, but we cannot presume that He has always let us in on the details.

Misguided prophetic speculation hurts the genuine study of biblical prophecy. Every time we run ahead of God, we leave some sincere believers behind questioning whether they can ever trust prophecy again. The ranks of post-tribulationists, amillennialists, postmillennialists and preterists is filled with disillusioned former pretribulationalists who gave up trying to figure out what God was really saying about the future.

God used specific predictions about the first coming of Christ, which were literally fulfilled in Jesus' life and ministry. The specific nature of these prophecies convinced us that Jesus was indeed the Promised One. St. Augustine said: "All these things are now seen to be fulfilled in accordance with the predictions which we read; and these fulfillments are now so many and so great that they lead us to await with confidence the fulfillment of the rest."[14]

If God pointed convincingly to the first coming of Christ, it only stands to reason that He has done the same regarding the second coming of Christ. Just as the first was literally fulfilled, so we believe the second will be as well. We look forward to His coming with great anticipation, "while we wait for the blessed hope—the glorious appearing of our great God and Savior, Jesus Christ" (Titus 2:13).

Miscalculating
the Second Coming

Eschatological excitement and prophetic panic tend to go hand in hand. Every time a war heats up in the Middle East, there will be a number of "prophetic panhandlers" assuring us that this is the big one. Despite the church's 20-century–long struggle to understand biblical prophecy, these modern-day "prophets" claim to have it all figured out—some to the very day!

As early as the second century, Christian "prophets," like Montanus, were proposing dates for the second coming of Christ. In A.D. 156 Montanus proclaimed to be an incarnation of the Holy Spirit and the revealer of "things to come." Gary DeMar points out that Montanus "proclaimed the imminent appearance of the New Jerusalem" and a "new outpouring of the Holy Spirit."[1] He was joined by two prophetesses, Prisca and Maximilla, in announcing the return of Christ to Phrygia in Asia Minor (modern Turkey). Their visions and prophecies were recorded in a "Third Testament" and were later rejected by the church as heretical.

Hippolytus (A.D. 170–236) went so far as to predict Christ would return in A.D. 500, based on the dimensions of Noah's ark.[2] In the third century, Novatian announced the imminent return of Christ, followed by Donatus in the fourth century. Donatus interpreted Revelation 14 as teaching that only 144,000 people would be saved when Jesus returned.[3] Later, the sack of Rome by the Vandals in A.D. 410 was viewed as a sure sign that the end was near.[4]

Millennial panic swept many parts of Europe as A.D. 999 came to an end. On New Year's Eve, Pope Sylvester II celebrated the last mass of the first millennium as A.D. 1000 approached. Russell Chandler notes that the pope himself believed this might be the last midnight mass of history. Taking a clue from the idea of the binding of Satan for 1,000 years, the pope and others concluded that the thousand years since the birth of Christ had now elapsed and Satan would again be loosed (see Revelation 20:7-8).

Russell Chandler says they viewed the dreaded eve of the new millennium as the "nightfall of the universe."[5] He observes that anxious crowds flooded the streets of Rome, while thousands of pilgrims "milled about hysterically" in Jerusalem, waiting for Christ to return to the holy city. Many had freed their slaves and paid off their debts to prepare for the final judgment. At midnight, the bells rang in the new millennium as a crowd dressed in sackcloth and ashes awaited the end of the world. But, alas, time marched on, and the second millennium of Church history became a reality.

Everything Old Is New Again

Most evangelicals hold the reformers and Puritans in high esteem as great theologians and expositors of the grace of God, and rightly so.[6] Therefore, it comes as a great surprise that their eschatological speculations were about as bizarre as any that may be offered today. However, given their historical frame of reference and certain *assumptions* of their times, it is easy to see how they developed *speculations* about the coming of Christ and the end of the world, which they thought could come at any moment.

Date-setting and speculation about the end times is an old habit. Many of the reformers believed they were living in the last days, that Satan had been loosed, and that the antichrist sought to extend his rule over the whole world by means of the Roman Catholic papacy. The idea had been developed during the Middle Ages that Satan was bound for a thousand years, approximately A.D. 300–1300. During this time, from the reign of Constantine until the time of the Reformation, the Gospel spread throughout Europe virtually unhindered.[7] Beginning in the twelfth century, prophetic pundits began to anticipate the rise of the antichrist around A.D. 1300.

Anselm of Havelburg (died 1158) was probably the first to suggest that the seven seals of Revelation represent the seven ages of church history. Otto of Freising (died 1158) predicted the thousand years of Satan's bondage would be followed by the final forty-two months of world history, culminating in the overthrow of the antichrist.[8]

John Wycliffe (1329–1384), often called the "Morning Star" of the Reformation, was extremely popular with the Puritans because he clearly identified the Catholic pope as the antichrist in his infamous work *De Papa*, published in 1379. He wrote: "The Pope is antichrist heere in erth, for he is agens [against] Christ both in life and in lore."[9] Thus Wycliffe has come to be viewed as the father of the Protestant apocalyptic tradition.

At the time of the Reformation, Martin Luther (1483–1546) was strongly influenced by Wycliffe's works, concluding that the pope was "the real Antichrist of whom all the Scripture speaks" in his *On the Papacy at Rome*. In 1529, amid his struggles with both the Roman Catholics and the radical Protestants, Luther discovered a late fifteenth-century commentary on the apocalypse by John Hilten, a Franciscan monk who identified the Turks with Magog and predicted an invasion of Germany by the Turks—a prospect that seemed a very real possibility in Luther's day. Interestingly, Hilten had also predicted that about 1516 a man would rise up, reform the church, and overthrow the papacy! Luther could not have helped being impressed by such a prediction. By November of that year, Luther had identified Gog as the Turks and Magog as the pope.[10]

John Calvin (1509–1564) is considered by many the greatest of the reformers. His *Institutes of the Christian Religion* (1536) were the first great theological works of the Reformation. He also wrote twenty-three commentaries and hundreds of letters, preached almost daily, and set up a Protestant haven at Geneva, Switzerland. He exerted considerable influence over John Knox, the Puritan exiles at Geneva, and the Duke of Somerset, protector of England during the reign of Edward VI.

Much more cautious than Luther in eschatology, Calvin deliberately avoided writing a commentary on Revelation. But in his commentary on 2 Thessalonians, he wrote: "The day of Christ will not come until the world has fallen into apostasy, and the rule of the Antichrist has held sway in the church." He viewed the antichrist not as the emperor nor as a single pope but as a succession of popes, stating, "all the marks by which the Spirit of God has pointed out antichrist appear clearly in the pope."[11]

John Bale (1495–1563), bishop, scholar, and English dramatist, wrote a commentary on the apocalypse, titled *The Image of Both Churches*.[12] He viewed the "woman in the wilderness" as the true church and the "whore of Babylon" as the Roman Catholic Church. He was also the first known writer to suggest there were seven periods of time covering the seven dispensations of human history. His importance in the history of dispensational thought has been almost entirely overlooked. It is obvious, however, that Bale's seven periods were the forerunners of the seven dispensations.

Even the Puritans Couldn't Get It Straight

Most of the reformers, like John Foxe (1516–1587) who wrote *Foxe's Book of Martyrs* (originally *Actes and Monuments*) believed that the Reformation was God's tool to rid England of the "agents of Babylon," namely the Catholic Church. Foxe's popularity convinced virtually the entire Church of England that the pope was the antichrist.

By 1560 the exiled Puritans at Geneva, Switzerland, had published the first annotated study Bible, known as the Geneva Bible. Having been exiled by the pro-Catholic "Bloody" Mary Tudor, their notes depicted the pope as the antichrist and the locusts from the bottomless pit as his agents: monks, friars, cardinals, patriarchs, and bishops. The Geneva Bible went through 140 printings and held popular sway over Protestant England even long after the *King James Version* appeared. Like many works at that time, it identified Babylon as symbolizing the Catholic Church and Magog (Ezekiel 28–29) as the Turks and Saracens.

The explorer Sir Walter Raleigh (1552–1618), who helped defeat the Spanish Armada in 1588, was a favorite of Queen Elizabeth I but fell into disfavor with King James, who imprisoned him in the Tower of London for thirteen years. There he wrote his famous *History of the Word*. He dated the creation at 4031 B.C. and divided history into three parts: before the law, under the law, and under grace. His views of prophecy led him to identify Magog as the Turks in the East and the Spaniards, "descendants of the Magogonians," in the West. He also pictured Muhammad as the "false prophet" of Revelation.[13]

One of the farthest-reaching predictions of the Puritan era was made by Hugh Broughton (1549–1612), who dated the creation at 3926 B.C. and added 6,000 years of human history, culminating in the return of Christ in A.D. 2072.[14] Needless to say, Broughton's view was not very popular because it put the second coming too far in the then-distant future. However, he still remains the only date-setter from that era that is yet to be proven wrong!

Rise of Mathematical Calculations

One of the most influential Puritan apocalyptists was John Napier (1550–1617) of Merchiston, Scotland.[15] He was recognized as one of the great minds of his day and is still remembered for the invention of logarithms in mathematics. He used his mathematical genius to fill his commentary on Revelation with maps, charts, and chronological tables. Ironically, his mathematical genius led to excessive prophetic speculation as he tried to uncover the mathematical framework of prophecy. Assuming Daniel's prophecy of "seventy weeks" (Daniel 9) is 490 years and then dividing in half, Napier surmised that every 245 years was significant in the rise and fall of empires.

Assuming that the trumpets and vials of Revelation were synonymous, Napier speculated that the fifth trumpet, "the star that fell," was Muhammad and the fifth vial, the "plague of locusts," was the rise of the Turks, which he dated at A.D. 1051, following Foxe's date. Working backward and forward from 1051, Napier devised this scheme based on 245-year intervals:

Trumpet & Vial	Event	Date
1	Destruction of Jerusalem	71
2	Eastern Empire established	316

Trumpet & Vial	Event	Date
3	Totila burns Rome	561
4	Charlemagne becomes emperor	806
5	Turks rise under Zadok	1051
6	Osman	1296
7	Reformation	1541

On the basis of his calculation, Napier said, "The last trumpet and vial beginneth *anno Christi* 1541 and should end in *anno Christi* 1786." He also predicted that 1639 would coincide with the third angel and usher in the final conflict between Christ (reformers) and antichrist (Rome). He saw the fourth angel as Christ Himself, who he predicted would return in 1688 and begin a harvest of the elect until 1786. He was also the first to suggest that the number of the antichrist, 666, could be found in the value of the Greek letters spelling *Lateinos,* which he associated with the Roman Catholic Church.

Napier's commentary was so popular it was published three times in Edinburgh (1593, 1611, and 1645) and twice in London (1594 and 1611). It was also printed twice in Dutch, five times in French, and three times in German. It was later abridged and reissued as *The Bloody Almanack* (1643 and 1647), which became the most powerful apocalyptic work of the English Civil War period, convincing Oliver Cromwell's followers that the final apocalypse had already begun and that they had put the antichrist to flight.

The Dating Game

From the first appearance of Napier's commentary, the prophetic dating game got into full swing. Napier was a mathematical genius and lent credibility to such an enterprise. Soon

Robert Pont (1524–1606), John Knox's son-in-law, tried to relate prophecy to astronomy in his chronological work *A newe treatise on the right reckoning of the yeares and ages of the world*, which appeared in 1599. He was the first reformer to suggest that six millennia (6,000 years) of human history would be followed by a seventh millennium of peace on earth. Interested in the stars, he speculated that the comet of 1572 was a sign from the Lord, like the star of Bethlehem heralding the end of the age, and that the eclipse of 1598 had ushered in the final darkness of the end times.

Thomas Brightman (1557–1607) was a Puritan pastor and scholar. His *Revelation of the Revelation*, published in 1609 after his death, became the most popular prophetic tract of Puritan England.[16] Brightman compared the seven churches of Revelation 2 and 3 to the seven ages of church history, suggesting that their distances from Ephesus paralleled the lengths of their ages. He suggested the following scheme:

Church	*Prophetic Period*
1. Ephesus	Apostles to Constantine
2. Smyrna	Constantine to Gratian (382)
3. Pergamum	382–1300
4. Thyatira	1300–1520
5. Sardis	German Reformation
6. Philadelphia	Genevan Reformation
7. Laodicea	Church of England

Brightman also introduced the idea of double fulfillments; thus the fifth trumpet referred to both Muhammad in the East and Pope Boniface III in the West. In the East the "locusts" were Saracens, while in the West they were monks and friars. The persecuted woman (Revelation 12) was the persecuted church from 300 to 1300, which was served by four "angels": Wycliffe, Hus, Luther, and Calvin. Brightman followed earlier commentators in believing Satan had been bound 1,000 years (300–1300) by Constantine, but had broken his shackles and was determined to destroy the true church by a conspiracy between the pope and the Turks.

Brightman believed that the last great "harvest" was brought about by Luther, the "avenging angel" was Thomas Cromwell, and the "soul under the altar" was the martyred Thomas Cranmer. He pictured the seven vials beginning under Queen Elizabeth I in 1560 with the first blast of the seventh trumpet. He offered the following scheme:

Vial One	(1563)	Elizabeth dismissed papal clergy.
Vial Two	(1564)	Council of Trent confirmed the damnation of nonelect.
Vial Three	(1581)	Act of Parliament against papists.
Vial Four	(present)	"Boiling heat of the sun is now every day to be looked for … whereby the man of sin may be vehemently scorched."
Vial Five	(by 1650)	Fall of Rome (pope).
Vial Six	(future)	Conversion of the Jews.
Vial Seven	(no later than 1695)	Battle of Armageddon.

Millennial Expectation

Puritan England's leading premillennialist was Joseph Mede (1586–1638).[17] He was one of the outstanding intellectuals of his day, combining the skills of a theologian, linguist, historian, and mathematician. A professor of Greek at Cambridge, Mede wrote an extensive commentary, *The Key to Revelation* (1627) and a shorter work, *The Apostasy of the Latter Times*, which appeared after his death in 1642. In his works he surmised that the 1,260 days, 42 months, and 3½ years of Revelation all referred to the same time period, which he took to mean 1,260 prophetic years. Rejecting the idea that Satan was bound by Constantine's legitimization of the church, Mede argued that Constantine's legalization of Christianity destroyed its original purity and ushered in an era of 1,260 years of apostasy from A.D. 395 to 1655. He predicted the fall of the beast (Roman church) in 1655, after which the "woman" (church) would return from the wilderness to take her proper place in the millennial reign of Christ.

In many ways Mede was the forerunner of later dispensational eschatology. He believed in the literal return of Christ, a 1,000-year reign of peace on earth, two judgments separated by the 1,000 years and the reign of the bride of Christ during the millennium. He differed with later dispensationalists on the unique position of the church, not Israel, during the millennium, but he did believe in the future conversion of the Jews, who would evangelize the world and rebuke the Church of Rome for its paganism.

Mede's influence was incredible. Like Napier before him, he brought intellectual authority to the study of prophecy. He taught such great men as John Milton, Isaac Newton, Jeremiah Burroughs, and Nathaniel Holmes. He also influenced the Puritan Thomas Goodwin, who succeeded him as England's leading premillennialist. Mede also corresponded extensively with Bishop James Ussher, whose chronology of dates was included in the original *Scofield Reference Bible* (1909).

As millennial expectation rose, so did militant Puritanism. Thomas Goodwin (1600–1680) and Jeremiah Burroughs (1559–1646) were nonconformist Congregationalists who advocated the literal interpretation of prophetic passages.[18] Suffering persecution under Archbishop William Laud of Canterbury, they radicalized the Puritan view of prophecy calling for the expulsion of King Charles I and Archbishop Laud as agents of the antichrist. Viewing themselves as the faithful witnesses of the last days, they called for the expulsion of the antichrist from the Church of England. Playing off the number 666, Goodwin argued that the antichrist's power would reach its peak in 1666, to be followed by the fall of the papacy and the Turkish Empire before 1700.

For most of the Puritans, millennial dawn seemed just around the corner with the outbreak of the English Civil War in 1642. The Westminster Assembly convened to rewrite Anglican theology in 1643; Archbishop Laud was executed for treason in 1645; and Charles I was executed as well in 1649. Even the great Puritan scholar John Owen could not resist calling his execution a fulfillment of prophecy in his sermon to Parliament the next day.[19] The British "moral majority" was in full control of England's destiny. But it was not long until the Puritans began arguing among themselves and calling each other the antichrist, and their movement collapsed. Cromwell died in 1658, and the monarchy was restored in 1660. By 1662 the Act of Uniformity had ejected more than 2,000 Puritan pastors from their pulpits and millennial expectation crashed into the bitter reality of political defeat.

Prophetic speculation continued during the eighteenth century, as any reading of Jonathan Edwards' *History of Redemption* will reveal, but it took a milder turn, and many of the old Puritan works went out of print—forever!

In the meantime, Pierre Poiret (1646–1719), a French philosopher, wrote about the seven dispensations in his *L'O Economie Divine,* published in Amsterdam in 1687 and translated into English in 1713. In 1699 John Edwards published *A Complete History or Survey of All the Dispensations* and the hymn writer and theologian Isaac Watts (1674–1748) laid out seven dispensations in his essay "The Harmony of All the Religions Which God Ever Prescribed to Men and All His Dispensations Towards Them."[20]

But it was not until the writings of John Nelson Darby (1800–1882) and the Plymouth Brethren in England, in the nineteenth century, that prophetic expectation would reach a new crescendo.

The Plymouth Brethren

Darby had left the Church of England because of his strong personal commitment to the Scriptures and joined a group of "Brethren" in the winter of 1827–1828 at Dublin, Ireland. They were a simple group of believers who broke bread every Lord's Day and believed in the liberty of ministry as a calling of God and not the ordination of man. He later moved to Plymouth, England in 1831, where his teachings about Bible prophecy flourished. Followers included such prominent men as George Muller of Bristol and numerous biblical scholars, including George Wigram and Samuel Tregelles.[21]

Darby and other Plymouth Brethren adopted a scheme of *seven dispensations* of God's economy in human history that were similar to those of Isaac Watts:

1. Paradise to the flood
2. Noah to Abraham
3. Abraham to Moses
4. Israel
5. Gentiles
6. The Spirit
7. The Millennium[22]

Unique to the teachings of Darby and the Brethren was the emphasis on the pretribulation rapture of the church. They believed that Christ would come to rapture ("translate") His bride, the true church, out of the world before the tribulation period began. Thus, the pretribulation rapture became the cornerstone of their eschatology, which viewed the tribulation as a time of divine judgment necessary to bring about the conversion of the Jews and the downfall of the antichrist.

Darby's teaching greatly influenced others, like W.E. Blackstone, whose popular book *Jesus Is Coming* was published in 1878; G. Campbell Morgan (1864–1945), who became one of England's greatest dispensational pastors and authors; and evangelist Dwight L. Moody of Chicago, who touched the world with his preaching. Their combined influence was also felt in the Bible conference movement of the nineteenth century, where many of the prophetic themes that influence the evangelical church today were developed. In time, other dispensational teachers rose to prominence, including A.J. Gordon of Boston and James H. Brookes of St. Louis.

Laodicean Liberals

While dispensationalists emphasized the imminent return of Christ to rapture the church at any moment, they were generally careful not to set any dates. However, it was common among dispensationalists to view the seven churches of Revelation as predicting the seven ages of church history in the following manner:[23]

1. Ephesus	Apostolic Age, 30–100
2. Smyrna	Persecuted Church, 100–300
3. Pergamum	Roman Church, 300–1200
4. Thyatira	Medieval Church, 1200–1500
5. Sardis	Reformation Church, 1500–1700
6. Philadelphia	Missionary Church, 1700–1900
7. Laodicea	Apostate Church, 1900–?

While no dates were set for the second coming of Christ in this scheme, the very fact that prophecy preachers paralleled Laodicea to the rise of theological liberalism in the mainline churches created the impression that the church stood at the end

of the Church Age and apostasy was already at work. The popularity of this idea was spread by the enormous reception given to
C.I. Scofield's (1843–1921) *Scofield Reference Bible*, originally published in 1909. Like many of the Puritans and Plymouth Brethren
before them, America's twentieth-century premillennialists
eagerly look forward in anticipation to the second coming of
Christ to set up His kingdom on earth.

Cultic Confusion

All of this is quite remarkable in light of some of the classic
millenarian schemes that tragically failed. In the 1820s Joseph
Smith, founder of the Mormons, claimed to have been visited by
an angel named Moroni, who directed him to discover and translate the golden tablets of *The Book of Mormon,* which was first
published in 1830. That same year the Church of Jesus Christ of
Latter-day Saints was officially organized. Smith's followers
believed they were living in the last days when Christ would
return to set up His millennial kingdom on earth for His saints,
at Salt Lake City, Utah.

In the meantime, William Miller, a Baptist pastor in Vermont,
assumed that the "2,300 days" from the transgression of the sanctuary to the cleansing of the sanctuary, mentioned in Daniel 8:14,
could be calculated as 2,300 years and could be dated from the
proclamation to rebuild the Jerusalem Temple in 457 B.C. By
adding 2,300 years he predicted that Christ would return literally
in 1843. He later refined the date to October 22, 1844. When
the day of "Great Disappointment" came, Miller gave up the
whole idea, but many of his followers refused to do so and
adopted the idea that on that date Christ moved into the Holy of
Holies in the heavenly temple to begin His atonement for our
sins. Thus, the Seventh Day Adventist movement began and has
grown to considerable size and influence with its insistence on

Saturday (Sabbath) worship in rejection of the "mark of the Beast," which they viewed as Sunday worship.

Toward the end of the nineteenth century, Charles Russell began to predict the return of Christ to establish His kingdom on earth in 1914. He published voluminously, including *Zion's Watch Tower* magazine and a lengthy series entitled *Millennial Dawn* (later called *Studies in Scripture*). When Christ did not return visibly in 1914, Russell's followers assumed He had returned secretly, revealing Himself only to Jehovah's Witnesses, as they called themselves, believing they were the 144,000 faithful witnesses of the apocalypse. Presuming the Church Age to have ended, they began meeting in "Kingdom Halls" to practice their faith.[24]

Viewing Prophecy Through Our Own Eyes

Perhaps the greatest problem for the church in the matter of interpreting biblical prophecy is the desire to view it through our own experience. The German theologians call this a *zeitgeist,* a current mood or response to certain existing conditions.[25] Unfortunately, as we have seen in this brief history of eschatological speculation, this has happened more often than not. The great temptation in prophetic interpretation is to move from the facts to our own *assumptions* and *speculations.*

The twentieth century is loaded with examples of prophetic speculations that never came true. It was *assumed* that ours must be the last age and that in the last days the antichrist will form an alliance of European nations and attack Israel. Here is just a sample of the proposals that were offered:

1. *Kaiser Wilhelm and the New Roman Empire*

The German emperor's title meant "Caesar." He intended to conquer all of Europe and reunite the old Roman Empire. Even the popular American evangelist Billy Sunday bought this idea, often saying: "If you turn hell upside down, you'll find 'made in Germany' stamped on the bottom!" The Kaiser's rise to power and his attempt to reunite Europe failed, and Germany was soundly defeated in Word War I.

2. Woodrow Wilson and the League of Nations

After the "Great War," as they called it then, the American president led an effort to establish the League of Nations as an international forum to prevent future world wars.

3. Benito Mussolini and the Fascist Revolt

The Italian strongman from Rome rose to power in 1922 as head of Italy's Fascist Party government. Immediately, prophetic speculators tagged him as the antichrist. Prophecy teachers quickly pointed out that the fascist symbol appeared on the back of the American dime—a "proof" of the antichrist's global rule. In 1929, Mussolini signed a concordat with the pope, furthering prophetic speculation. But in the end, Mussolini committed suicide as Italy fell to the allies in World War II.

4. Adolph Hitler and World War II

Hitler has become the ultimate personification of evil. No one in the twentieth century was a better "candidate" to be the antichrist. He rose to power in Germany as the head of the Nazi Party. He promised to resurrect Germany from its defeat in World War I and make her great again—and, if necessary, by force. When Germany signed a nonaggression pact with Russia in 1939, prophecy pundits immediately tagged the duo as "Gog and Magog." But in 1941, Hitler turned against the communists and invaded Russia. Hitler formed a murderous alliance with Mussolini and turned his hand against everyone. In the process, he persecuted and murdered 6 million Jews. But in the end, Hitler himself was dead and Germany was in ashes.

5. *Joseph Stalin and the Soviet Union*

The atheistic leader of the Soviet Union was our ally in World War II, but it was an uneasy alliance at best. Some prophecy buffs had Stalin labeled as the "man of sin" long before and after Hitler. Others were convinced that Russia was the Magog of Ezekiel's prophecy (Ch. 38–39). After Stalin's death, Krushchev, Andropov, Breshnev and even Gorbachev were all suggested as possible candidates for the antichrist. A few even suggested that Gorbachev's birthmark was the "mark of the beast!" When the Soviet Union dissolved in 1991, prophecy speculators were left guessing about the future of Russia.

6. *John F. Kennedy and the "Deadly Wound"*

Anti-Catholic fundamentalists were certain that America's first Roman Catholic president was the antichrist himself. They predicted a world alliance among Kennedy, the pope, Martin Luther King Jr., and the communists to take over the world. In 1963, Kennedy was tragically assassinated and prophetic speculation shifted to various world leaders. Key choices included Henry Kissinger (he was Jewish); Ronald Wilson Reagan (he had six letters in each of his three names); Juan Carlos of Spain (he descended from Roman emperors) and Prince Charles of England (based on his supposed descent from the "lost" tribe of Dan). In the meantime, some even insisted that Kennedy was only mortally wounded and would recover from his "deadly wound" in fulfillment of Revelation 13:3. Others pointed out that President Reagan and Pope John Paul II had also recovered from deadly wounds and might rise to even greater power.

7. NATO, the Common Market and the European Union

Prophecy students have interpreted various attempts to unify Europe as a sign of the last days. The formation of NATO (North Atlantic Treaty Organization) in 1949 caught attention immediately after World War II. The 1957 signing of the Rome Treaty calling for the European Common Market—later called the European Economic Community (EEC) and today called the European Union (EU)—have always been targets of prophetic speculation. The recent implementation of the Maastricht Treaty in 1991 further fueled such speculation. All of this sounds like the reunification of Europe is a very real possibility in our lifetime, but only time will tell how successful these efforts will be in that direction.[26]

8. Bill Gates, Computers and the World Wide Web

One of the more recent prophetic speculations has been that Bill Gates of Microsoft, the richest man in the world, is the antichrist. Some have even pointed out that much of the lingo of the computerized world of visual reality is linked to terms like icon (Greek word for "image" of the Beast). More and more, prophecy pundits are looking at modern technology and its possible role in the fulfillment of end times prophecies. Computerized images, satellite transmissions, point-of-sale terminals, credit cards, digital imaging and implanted computer chips are all candidates for the "mark of the beast."

The real tragedy is that instead of rejecting prophetic speculation for what it is, we are often duped by it. People guessing dates and selecting candidates for the antichrist are claiming to know more than the writers of Scripture did, and that is always dangerous. Dr. Daniel Mitchell writes: "Speculating on the date of Christ's return not only breeds bad theology, but it is the original sin all over again—trying to know as much as God."[27] He goes on to note that the expectation of Christ's return *at any moment* has been a source of hope and comfort to the church since the days of the apostles. Any apparent delay is not due to God's indecision but to the fact that He has not let us in on the secret!

I believe the Bible clearly predicts the rise of a personal antichrist at the end of human history, but I doubt we will ever know who he is until it is too late. The apostle Paul said of him, "don't let anyone deceive you in any way, for that day will not come until the rebellion occurs and the man of lawlessness ["man of sin," KJV] is revealed, the man doomed to destruction" (2 Thessalonians 2:3). Paul reminds us that the "power of lawlessness" (2 Thessalonians 2:7) is already at work, but it will eventually culminate when the lawless one is revealed (2 Thessalonians 2:8).

In the meantime, we are admonished to "stand firm" and hold to the doctrine of the apostles of our Lord (2 Thessalonians 2:15) that we might be strengthened "in every good deed and word" (2 Thessalonians 2:17). Thus, Paul's advice to us is the same as that of the Lord Jesus who told us to watch, stay ready, and keep serving until He comes (Matthew 24:42-46).

When you study the *facts* of prophecy, be sure that you distinguish them from the *assumptions* you draw or the *speculations* you make. While we would all like to believe that our Lord will come in our lifetime, it is presumption to assume that we are the terminal generation. Surely, He could come today, but He may not come for many years. That decision is up to God the Father.

Jesus Never Set a Date for His Return

Questions about the second coming of Christ and the end of the world are not new. Jesus' own disciples raised three such questions themselves. Toward the end of His earthly ministry, Jesus predicted the destruction of Jerusalem and the Temple. Matthew 24–25 contains Jesus' last major discourse and His clearest statements about the future. His message included a prediction of the imminent fall of Jerusalem and also pointed to the distant future when the "times of the Gentiles" would come to an end during the great tribulation.

The disciples were awed by the spectacular architecture of the temple in Jerusalem and commented on it to Jesus. To their amazement, He replied that "not one stone here will be left on another; every one will be thrown down" (Matthew 24:2). Stunned by this remark, the disciples asked their Lord three questions:

1. "When will this happen?"

2. "What will be the sign of your coming?"

3. "And of the end of the age?"(Matthew 24:3)

As He sat on the Mount of Olives, opposite the temple precincts, Jesus answered those questions in what has been called the Olivet Discourse. Thus, His entire message is looked on as the answer to these three questions. John Walvoord comments, "Premillenarians, accordingly, interpret the discourse as an accurate statement of end-time events, which will lead up to and climax in the second coming of Christ to set up His millennial kingdom on earth."[1]

The key to interpreting this passage rests in one's view of the "gospel of the kingdom" (Matthew 24:13-14). Since Matthew has already shown in his parables that the present form of the kingdom is the church, it seems proper to interpret the events in this discourse as relating to the entire Church Age and culminating during the tribulation period. Thus, the "signs" (Greek, *semeion*) of the end are general characteristics of the present age, which shall be intensified as this age moves toward its conclusion. These are followed by more specific signs (Matthew 24:15-26) of the tribulation period and the final return of Christ in judgment (Matthew 24:27-31).

Signs of the Times

Jesus warned His followers not to be deceived by the host of false prophets and false messiahs who would follow in a long parade throughout the Church Age. He also warned of "wars and rumors of wars" (Matthew 24:6) that would follow throughout the present era and that have continually marked the "age of the Gentiles." Such wars do *not* in themselves indicate that the end is near. These are only the "beginning of birth pains" (Matthew

24:8). Such conflicts may point to the end, but serious Bible students dare not interpret any one conflict as necessarily "prophetic" of the end times. In reality, every war that occurs on earth during this present era is a fulfillment of this prophecy.

Despite such wars, Jesus warned in Matthew 24:6, "The end is still to come" ("the end is not yet" [KJV]). Unfortunately, many people miss this point altogether. They read about wars, earthquakes, and natural disasters and conclude that the end must be near. Yet Jesus Himself said such is not the case.

Thus the Persian Gulf War cannot be viewed as necessarily a fulfillment of prophecy, though it may be a step in that direction. This is precisely where Bible students need to be careful not to jump from the *facts* of prophecy to their well-intended *assumptions* and finally to pure *speculations*.

Everything listed in this part of Jesus' response—wars, famines, and earthquakes—is to be expected throughout the Church Age until He returns. These are the "beginning of birth pains" (Matthew 24:8), but they do not in themselves prove the final fulfillment is about to be delivered.

Every crisis in the Middle East—1948, 1956, 1967, 1973, and 1991—has led to similar prophetic speculations, with sincere teachers announcing that the end is just around the corner. What the recent crisis shows is that the old animosities have not died out, and the potential for a major Arab alliance against Israel in the last days is still a very real possibility in the future—but that future could be a month, a year, ten years, or a hundred years from now.

The End of the Age

Jesus stated that the end of the age would come when the "gospel of the kingdom" has been preached in the whole world as a testimony to all nations (Matthew 24:14). The proclamation of

the gospel is not precisely defined as to whether it is *announced* to
all the world (Greek, *oikoumene*, "inhabited world") and every
nation (Greek, *ethnos*, "Gentile nations") or whether it is *believed*
in every nation. But one fact is clear: Christ's Great Commission
to evangelize the world (Matthew 28:18-20) is to be carried out
faithfully until He returns. Christ's later warning (Matthew
24:36) that no one knows the time of His return emphasizes that
we are to continue faithfully doing what He commanded until
He comes.

The end (Greek, *telos*) that shall come after the proclamation
of the gospel is the end of the Church Age, which parallels the
"times of the Gentiles" during the present era. While some commentators limit the events in this passage to the tribulation
period, it seems clear that they are occurring throughout the
entire Church Age as the gospel is preached primarily to the
Gentiles.[2]

Eschatology is the study of the end times and is generally associated with the study of biblical prophecies of future events. Jesus
spoke of the "end of the age" in response to His disciples' questions. There can be no doubt that He viewed human history as
moving toward a final climax, not as an endless cycle of repetitious
events. William S. LaSor notes that the Jews of the intertestamental period distinguished between "this age" (Hebrew, *hauolam
hazzeh*) and "the age to come" (Hebrew, *hauolam habbah*). Thus,
LaSor concludes that the expression "the end of the world" comes
from Judeo-Christian roots and is understood by both Jews and
Christians as referring to this world (or age) coming to an end
and being replaced by the age to come.[3]

A similar concept is found in the Old Testament expression
"the latter days" (Hebrew, *beaharit hayyamim)*. Moses foretold the
future apostasy of Israel, her scattering, and her return to the Lord
in the "latter days" (Deuteronomy 4:30; cf. 31:29, KJV). The
prophet Hosea spoke of the future repentance of Israel in the

"latter days" (Hosea 3:5 KJV). The prophet Jeremiah predicted numerous events that would occur in the "latter days" (Jeremiah 23:20; 30:24; 48:47; 49:39 KJV). Ezekiel predicted the invasion of Israel by a coalition of nations ("Gog and Magog") in the "latter days" (Ezekiel 38:16 KJV), also using the alternate expression "in the latter years" (Ezekiel 38:8 KJV).

It was against this Old Testament backdrop that our Lord spoke to His disciples about the coming end of the world. His warnings about false prophets, counterfeit messiahs, natural disasters, and persecution have proven true time and time again throughout the Church Age.

The Great Tribulation

As Jesus looked down the corridor of time to the end of the present age—an age that would be launched by the preaching of the gospel of His death and resurrection and by the empowerment of His disciples with the Holy Spirit—He warned of a time of great tribulation ("great distress" [Matthew 24:21 NIV]) which would come upon the whole world (Matthew 24:15-28). The "abomination of desolation" (Matthew 24:15 KJV) refers to when Antiochus Epiphanes profaned Jewish temple worship during the intertestamental period (Daniel 9:27; 11:31; 12:11), foreshadowing an even more serious abomination that would yet occur in the future. Whereas Antiochus offered an unclean pig on the sacred altar of the temple, the antichrist will offer himself! (2 Thessalonians 2:4).

The act of desecration that Daniel had predicted about Antiochus, the pagan Hellenistic ruler, will be repeated even more seriously in the future as the signal of the beginning of the great tribulation on earth. Since Jesus saw this as still in the future, such an abomination is not limited to the past actions of Antiochus. Nor was it fulfilled merely in the Roman destruction of Jerusalem in A.D. 70, since our Lord called it the "great tribulation" (KJV) that is "unequaled from the beginning of the world until now— and never to be equaled again" (Matthew 24:21). Our Lord went on to explain that the devastation of the Great Tribulation will be so awful that unless those days were cut short, "no one would survive" (Matthew 24:22).

Jesus further described this coming time of trouble ("distress," NIV) as a time when the sun and moon are darkened and the heavens shall be shaken (Matthew 24:29). His description runs parallel to that found in Revelation 16:1-16, where the final hour of the earth's tribulation is depicted by atmospheric darkness, air pollution, and ecological disaster. These cataclysmic events accompany the return of Christ at the end of the tribulation period.

Christ's return to earth will be marked by "the sign of the Son of Man" appearing in the sky (Matthew 24:30). This sign is not explained in this passage. Ancient commentators, like Chrysostom, thought it might be the appearance of a cross in the sky. More recent commentators tend to follow Lange's view that it is the Shekinah glory of the divine Christ.[4]

How Soon Will It Be?

Jesus reminded His disciples that they could discern the coming of the end of the age by the illustration of a blossoming fig tree. Our Lord said, "Now learn this lesson from the fig tree: As soon as its twigs get tender and its leaves come out, you know that summer is near" (Matthew 24:32). When a tree blooms in the spring, we discern that summer is coming. "Even so," Jesus added, "when you see all these things, you know that it [My coming] is near, right at the door" (Matthew 24:33).

The immediate context is illustrative of the point our Lord was making about His coming. While Israel at times is symbolized as a fig tree, the usage here seems to be that of a general illustration. A parallel passage in Luke 21:29 refers to the "fig tree" and "all the trees." There is no indication in the immediate context that the fig tree is meant to symbolize the rebirth of Israel. Just as God has programmed time indicators into nature (e.g., budding trees), so He has programmed into prophetic history certain time indicators of future events.

The generation that lives to see "all these things" come to pass will "not pass away" before Christ returns at the end of the age (Matthew 24:34). This difficult saying has been variously interpreted as (1) being fulfilled in the apostles' own lifetime with the destruction of Jerusalem in A.D. 70; (2) referring to the perpetual survival of the race ("generation") of the Jews; (3) the terminal generation at the time of Christ's return. The Arndt and Gingrich lexicon prefers to translate "generation" (Greek, *genea*) as "age" or "period of time."[5] In other words, the previously listed signs will continue to multiply throughout the Church Age and reach their ultimate climax at the end of the age—in the generation of those who live to see the entire matter fulfilled.

The return of the Jewish people to the land of Israel began at the end of the nineteenth century and continued throughout the twentieth century. In 1948, the official establishment of the nation of Israel was recognized by the United Nations. Most prophecy students recognized this as a prophetically significant event. For many, it was the first "sign" to actually be fulfilled. One could argue that modern Israel could yet be expelled from the land and return again at some future date, but this is highly unlikely. After nineteen centuries of absence, it would seem that the reestablishment of Israel in 1948 does have prophetic significance.

One of the problems in attempting to date the sequence of coming events in relation to Israel is that a generation (forty years) has already passed (1948 + 40 = 1988). Some have suggested that the Jewish people did not acquire all of Jerusalem until 1967 and propose 2007 as the terminal date of a forty-year "generation." Others claim that the final generation will not begin until modern Israel acquires the full limit of ancient Israel's biblical borders. By this reckoning, the final countdown has not yet begun.

There is no clear biblical definition of the length of a generation. In Genesis 15:13-16, four generations totaled 400 years, making each generation 100 years in length. Someone is bound to point this out as we approach 2048 and suggest it as the terminal date for the return of Christ, with the rapture coming seven years earlier, in 2041.

In the meantime, the basic *facts* of Jesus' prophecy remain clear. There will come a generation that will see "all these things" fulfilled in its lifetime, and it will be the terminal generation of the Church Age. Attempts to limit "this generation" to the generation of Jesus' day remove any future predictive element from Jesus' prophecy and confine it to the destruction of Jerusalem in A.D. 70. This approach, often called *preterism* (indicating a past fulfillment) is hard pressed to explain how the gospel was preached to "all nations" before A.D. 70 (cf. Matthew 24:14) or how the "sign of the Son of man … coming in the clouds of heaven … to gather the elect" (Matthew 24:30-31) was fulfilled when the Roman army destroyed Jerusalem.[6]

The Timing of Christ's Return

Jesus Himself gave no clear indication of the timing of His second coming. In John 14:1-3, He promised the disciples that if He went to the "Father's house" (heaven) to "prepare a place" for them, He would come again for them. In Matthew 24:36, our Lord clearly stated that no one "but my Father only" knows the time of His return. If the angels don't know, we can safely assume

Satan doesn't know, and we can certainly be assured that people don't know *when* Jesus is coming.

The only possible hint that Christ might not come back for a long time appears in the parable of the talents (Matthew 25:14-30). In this illustration to the basic message of the Olivet Discourse, our Lord emphasizes the importance of faithful serving in His absence. The "talents" represent monetary values entrusted to us for use in God's service and symbolize the gifts and abilities He has given us with which to serve Him. The "far country" (Matthew 25:14 KJV) seems to be heaven. Notice, the master is gone "a long time" before returning to call his servants to accountability. The fearful servant who hid the money failed to understand the real generosity of the master who wanted him to experience the joys of service. The fact that Christ went to the "far country" (heaven) and was gone a "long time" is an indication to the disciples that He will not return any time soon.

Jesus and the Prophets

Jesus' predictions about the end times blend His answers to all three questions raised by His disciples. Obviously, the temple was destroyed by the Romans in A.D. 70, but the preaching of the gospel to the whole world is still in progress today. Thus, both a near judgment of Jerusalem by the Romans and an ultimate judgment by the antichrist seem to be in view in this passage. LaSor notes: "But regardless of the sequence intended (or that we impose on the passage), Jesus does mention a great tribulation in connection with the end time events."[7] He further notes that Jesus' reference to the prophet Daniel definitely connects Him to Israel's prophetic heritage.

Daniel's prophecies (Daniel 2 and 7) mention the sequence of four major Gentile world powers that will come in succession: Babylon, Persia, Greece, and Rome. Out of the latter kingdom one will rise who will make "war against the saints" (Daniel 7:19-21). He is also pictured as one who brings "desolation" and "abomination" (Daniel 9:27). (This same imagery is used by our Lord in the New Testament.) In Daniel 11:21-31 we read again of the "contemptible person" who profanes the temple with his armed forces to set up the "abomination that causes desolation." From the context of Daniel's prophecies, we conclude that the "time of trouble," or "great tribulation," involves Daniel's people, the Jews. We also conclude that the king who "magnifies himself above every God" (Daniel 11:36) is the antichrist of the last days.

The prophet Jeremiah also refers to a "time of trouble for Jacob [Israel]" (Jeremiah 30:1-9) in the future. Jeremiah was writing during the Babylonian captivity and saw in the distant future an even greater time of trouble.

The book of Revelation pictures the Great Tribulation as both Satan's last desperate attempt to destroy the work of God in creation and salvation and as God's ultimate judgment on the kingdom of Satan as the outpouring of the "wrath of the Lamb" (Revelation 6:16), who is Christ. The Great Tribulation is the final judgment of God against the sin and wickedness on earth and results in the resounding declaration, "It is done!" (literally, "It is finished," Revelation 16:17). The atonement of Christ was finalized with this same declaration on the cross, when He lifted up His head and with a loud voice said, "It is finished" (Matthew 27:50; John 19:30). Now, at the end of the great tribulation of God's judgment, the same cry will go up: "It is finished!"

The final act of God's judgment at the end of the Great Tribulation is generally referred to as the battle of Armageddon (Revelation 16:16). The other biblical term for this final conflict is the "day of the Lord," which is mentioned several times in the Old Testament prophets.[8] This "day" is viewed by the prophets as a day of darkness and judgment related to the end time.

The prophet Zechariah pictured the "day of the Lord" as a time when all the nations will gather together against the city of Jerusalem, and the Lord shall go forth to defend the city and "on that day His feet shall stand on the Mount of Olives, east of Jerusalem, and the Mount of Olives will be split in two from east to west, forming a great valley, with half of the mountain moving north and half moving south" (Zechariah 14:4).

Back to the Future

As we trace the words of Jesus back to the Old Testament prophets, we see that they all point to the future. In a very significant and symbolic gesture, Jesus took His disciples to the Mount of Olives to deliver His most important prophetic message. Not only could they look down on the city of Jerusalem and the temple across the Kidron Valley, but they were sitting on the very mount from which Jesus would ascend back into heaven (Acts 1:12) and to which He will one day return. He will split it in two when He comes to judge the world and deliver His people.

They could not have gone to a more appropriate place to receive Jesus' message about those things pertaining to His second coming and the end of the age. Think of what that mountain has witnessed over the years:

- The conquest of Jerusalem by King David of Israel (c. 1000 B.C.)

- David's retreat from Jerusalem and from Absalom over the Mount of Olives

- David's return to Jerusalem and the restoration of his throne

- The splendor of Jerusalem under King Solomon and the building of the Temple (971–931 B.C.)

- The subsequent rise and fall of the kings of Judah at Jerusalem (931–586 B.C.)

- The Babylonian captivity and the destruction of the Temple (586 B.C.)

- The Jews' return under Ezra and the rebuilding of the Temple by Zerubbabel (515 B.C.)

- Rebuilding of the walls of Jerusalem by Nehemiah (445 B.C.)

- The Temple repaired and expanded by Herod the Great (beginning in 20 B.C.)

- The ministry, death, and resurrection of Jesus Christ (A.D. 30–33)

- The Temple completed (A.D. 64)

- The destruction of Jerusalem and the Temple and the scattering of the Jews (A.D. 70)

- The rise of Islam and the building of the Dome of the Rock in honor of Muhammad (A.D. 687–691)

- General Allenby of Great Britain liberating Jerusalem from the Turks, and the beginning of the British protectorate of Palestine (A.D. 1917)

- Israel reestablished as a nation (A.D. 1948)

- Israel gaining full possession of Jerusalem (A.D. 1967)

Yet the greatest prophetic event of all is yet in the future—the return of Jesus Christ to the Mount of Olives! In His Olivet Discourse our Lord promised to return but set no date, though He implied in His illustrations that He would be gone for a long time (Matthew 25:5,19). He urged His disciples to always be ready for Him to return. Thus, the concept of an imminent and sudden, or unexpected, coming reminds us to "be ready" whenever He might return.

In the meantime, Jesus instructed His disciples to keep serving Him faithfully until He returned. This dual emphasis leaves us with a proper balance about matters of biblical prophecy, the return of Christ, and the end of the age. On the one hand, we are to be watching and ready for Him to come at any moment. On the other hand, we are to continue serving Him for as long as He waits. One preacher put it this way: "Live your life as though He could come today, but plan your work as if you had a hundred years."

The most serious announcement in Jesus' message was that *no one* can set any dates for His return (Matthew 24:36). Yet this has been one of the most violated declarations in Scripture. Over the centuries, well-meaning believers have wanted to assume they were living in the "last days." Something in the human psyche makes us want to believe we are the "terminal generation." Perhaps it is a combination of pride about ourselves and our excitement about the coming of Christ that causes us to read the prophecies of the future through the eyes of the present. But whenever believers have done this, they have jumped from the facts of prophecy to their own *assumptions* and eventually to wide-eyed *speculations*.

Whenever preachers start saying things like, "it will all be over in six years," they are speculating and not preaching. No one knows how long we have until Jesus comes. How many times have we heard or read some wide-eyed speculation about future events only to watch them fade into the sands of time? Does anyone object to such speculation or urge caution to such statements? Hardly at all! The problem with all this is that it causes thinking people to overreact against legitimate Bible prophecies and reject them altogether.

Guessing dates and reading our own times into biblical prophecy is a temptation to which Christians have often succumbed. The end is near, but we dare not claim to know that the end is here. Apocalyptic speculation is a difficult and dangerous enterprise when applied to political and social policies. One had better be sure he is right before proceeding with his vision for the end. If no one really knows when Jesus is coming, then simple logic would tell us: Don't waste your time trying to guess the time; be ready all the time, because Jesus could come at *any* time.

When I was in college thirty years ago, some students were theorizing that the days were short and the end was near. "Why not drop out now," they said, "and give our lives to serving God?" They missed the point that by studying they were serving God— and home they went. It has also occurred to me since then that if they had stayed in school, they might be better equipped today to have a really effective ministry for God.

If you have a job, keep it—don't quit. God may lead you to take a step of faith in His service, but don't take a step of foolishness. Over the years, I have watched many people give up all responsibility "to serve the Lord," only to watch them take it all back on themselves later. Be faithful in your tasks today and God will open doors of service tomorrow.

If you have a place of service in your local church, keep at it— don't quit. If you are a teacher, keep teaching. If you are in choir, keep singing. If you are an elder, keep ruling. If you are a deacon, keep serving. And if you are a pastor, keep pastoring. As the hymn writer has so beautifully said it: "May He find us faithful when He comes."

Beware of
False Prophets

Spiritual deception is as old as Satan. He deceived himself into thinking that he could rebel against God and get away with it. Ever since his fateful fall, Satan has been deceiving anyone who would listen to his lies.

False prophets are really the emissaries of Satan. Their preaching distorts and denies the truth of God and puts their followers into spiritual bondage.[1]

A false prophet is one who contradicts the true message of Christ, as well as one whose predictions fail to come true. David Koresh was guilty on both counts. A typically self-deceived extremist cult leader, Koresh perished with nearly 90 of his followers in the flames of "Ranch Apocalypse." And in Matthew 23:27-33, Jesus Christ warned there is a worse fate for false prophets: They will not escape the fires of hell!

Jesus spoke often of false prophets and spiritual deception. He told His disciples that spiritual truth could be recognized by its fruits. Then He added, "Not everyone who says to me, 'Lord, Lord,' will enter the kingdom of heaven….Many will say to me on that day, 'Lord, Lord, did we not prophesy in your name, and in your name drive out demons and perform many miracles?' Then I will tell them plainly, 'I never knew you. Away from me, you evildoers!'" (Matthew 7:21-23).

One might expect false prophets and extremist cults to arise from non-Christian religions that reject Jesus Christ. But when false cults arise from within Christianity, it is especially disturbing. The New Testament, however, is filled with warnings about heretics, false prophets and false prophecies. Even in apostolic times, the apostle John wrote, "Dear children, this is the last hour; and as you have heard that the antichrist is coming, even now many antichrists have come….They went out from us, but they did not really belong to us" (1 John 2:18,19).

Masters of Deceit

The Bible describes Satan as the "father of lies" (John 8:44). He is pictured in Scripture as the ultimate deceiver; his name means "accuser." He is the accuser of God and His people (Revelation 12:10). He is opposed to God and seeks to alienate people from the truth. He misled the fallen angels (Matthew 25:41; Revelation 12:4). He tempts men and women to sin (Genesis 3:1-13; 1 Timothy 6:9). He denies and rejects the truth of God and deceives those who are perishing without God (2 Thessalonians 2:10). Ultimately, he "inspires" the false prophets and the very spirit of antichrist (1 John 2:18-23).

The Bible clearly warns us that in the last days people will "abandon the faith and follow deceiving [seducing, KJV] spirits and things [doctrines, KJV] taught by demons" (1 Timothy 4:1).

These false teachings will come through hypocritical liars whose minds have been captured by Satan's lies. Thus, the process of spiritual deception is clearly outlined in Scripture:

The term *angel* (Greek, *angelos*) means "messenger." God's angels are His divine messengers (Hebrews 1:14; Revelation 1:1), and His true prophets and preachers are called the angels of the churches (Revelation 2:1,8,12,18; 3:1,7,14). By contrast, Satan is pictured as a fallen angel, the leader of other fallen angels and the one who deceives the whole world (Revelation 12:9). He is revealed as the ultimate power behind the antichrist and the false prophet, who deceives mankind with false religion (Revelation 13:14). Thus, the messengers of deceit are Satan-inspired false prophets and teachers whose messages are the very spirit of antichrist (1 John 2:18).

The Process of Deception

The lure of false doctrine is that it presents itself as the truth. It appears as a corrective measure to established doctrine. It is propagated by those who are certain they have discovered some new revelation of truth or a better interpretation of old, established truth. Either way, they are convinced they are right and everyone else is wrong.

That is Satan's oldest trick. He appeals to our *self-conceit* and leads us into *self-deceit*. When he first approached Eve, Satan questioned the integrity of God's command and appealed to her selfish desire to be like God. It was that same desire that had led to his own fall in the first place. And there is something selfish enough in all of us to want to believe that we can know what no one else knows. C.S. Lewis said,

> What Satan put into the heads of our remote ancestors was the idea that they could "be like gods."... And out of that hopeless attempt has come nearly all that we can call human history... the long terrible story of man trying to find something other than God which will make him happy.[2]

One does not have to look hard to find expression of self-centeredness in most cult leaders: Father Divine said he was God. David Koresh claimed to be Jesus Christ. Sun Myung Moon says he is "Lord of the Universe." Joseph Smith claimed to receive angelic revelations. Mary Baker Eddy believed her book, *Key to the Scriptures,* was inspired of God. Herbert W. Armstrong claimed his church was the only one on earth proclaiming "the very same gospel that Jesus taught and proclaimed."

Once the false teacher falls into the illusion that he or she alone is God's messenger and has a corner on His truth, spiritual deception is inevitable. Mary Baker Eddy, the founder of Christian Science, was so convinced she was right that she said, "Today the healing power of Truth is widely demonstrated as an imminent, eternal science....[Its] coming as was promised by the Master is for its establishment as a permanent dispensation among men."[3] She believed that her "discovery" of Christian Science fulfilled the promise of Jesus' second coming!

In the preface to her *Key to the Scriptures,* Mrs. Eddy said of herself, "Since the author's discovery of the might of Truth in the treatment of disease as well as of sin, her system has been fully tested and has not been found wanting."[4] It is difficult to imagine the sincerity of such self-conceit and spiritual arrogance. The only logical explanation is that she really thought she was right.

Once *spiritual deception* sets in, it leads to *spiritual darkness.* It is not long before the deceived cult leader begins to espouse heretical doctrine. Since he or she acknowledges no one else as God's spokesperson, traditional and orthodox concepts may be challenged or even disregarded. Pride and arrogance are the sins that lead a person to become spiritually deceived. These sins take us to the second stage of spiritual deception. Satan tempts us with our own self-centeredness and lures us into spiritual darkness with the bait of our own pride. We really want to believe we are right and everybody else is wrong. The Bible calls it the "pride of life" (1 John 2:16 NASB).

Having been hooked by our arrogance, we are reeled in by our ignorance. Most people who fall into the trap of false doctrine are ignorant of the implications of their views. Hank Hanegraaff illustrates this in his epic work *Christianity in Crisis.*[5] In exposing serious doctrinal flaws, Hanegraaff states that many sincere preachers get off the theological track, but don't know enough theology to realize their error.

The problems arise when false teachers love their erroneous teachings to the point they will not repent of them even when their error is exposed. This is what leads to *spiritual blindness.* The willful rejection of the truth results in the mind being blinded by Satan. The Bible says, "They are darkened in their understanding and separated from the life of God because of the ignorance that is in them due to the hardening of their hearts" (Ephesians 4:18).

Scripture further explains that Satan himself is the source of spiritual darkness: "The god of this age has blinded the minds of unbelievers, so that they cannot see the light of the gospel of the glory of Christ, who is the image of God" (2 Corinthians 4:4).

Once theological error falls into "ecclesiastical cement" it is virtually impossible to eliminate it. When false doctrine is accepted by an organized religious body, it will be perpetrated by a false defense (apologetic) based upon a false premise. If I honestly believe my dog is a reincarnation of my Uncle Joe, I will look for every possible proof of Uncle Joe's personality in my dog's behavior. When a whole group of followers accept false doctrine as truth, they will organize it, categorize it and systematize it. But that doesn't make it true!

The Cultic Paradigm

All cult logic is built on the same faulty premise: "We alone know the truth." Believing themselves to have discovered truth that is unknown to others, cultists assume they have a corner on that truth. The cultic paradigm works like this:

> We alone know the truth of God;
> therefore,
> we alone are the people of God.

Other variations of the cultic paradigm derive from this original premise. For example, if we alone know the truth, then all others are in error. If we alone are the people of God, then all others are heretics. If people reject our message, they are rejecting God's message. If people persecute us, they are persecuting the cause of God because our cause is God's cause. Since we are right, and others are wrong, our church is the only true church.

While schismatic cults exist in every religion from Lubavitcher Jews to Muslim extremists, they all have certain characteristics in common.

1. *Extrabiblical Revelation*

Every religious cult has a sacred book translation, set of writings, key to interpretation, and perhaps visions, dreams or voices to validate its beliefs. Muslims believe the Koran is God's final revelation to man through the Prophet Muhammed. Mormons look at *The Book of Mormon* as equally inspired as the Bible. Jehovah's Witnesses recognize only their New World Translation of the Bible. Seventh-day Adventists recognize Ellen G. White as an inspired prophet of God. Christian Science reveres Mary Baker Eddy's *Science and Health with Key to the Scriptures* as divinely inspired.

While some cultic religions have gone so far as to produce and sanction their own sacred books, others have not. Instead, they claim allegiance to the Bible, but insist that their interpretation is the only spiritually valid understanding of Scripture. The Way International founder Victor Paul Wierwille claims, "God spoke to me audibly, just like I'm talking to you now. He said he would teach me the word as it had not been known since the first century."[6] By contrast, *The Way* magazine condemns the so-called Christian church as being built essentially upon manmade doctrine and tradition.[7] Thus, Josh McDowell and Don Stewart conclude, "The Way International believes Victor Paul Wierwille has the only true interpretation of the Scriptures and is the only one who can lead fellow Bible students out of the confusion in which traditional Christianity has engulfed them."[8]

The Children of God (COG), also known as the Family of Love, recognize David Berg as "prophet and King" and his "Mo letters" as God's truth. Berg himself has said, "My letters mean exactly what they say, literally, and they don't need explaining away, spiritualizing or reinterpreting by any one."[9] One of Berg's early prophecies concerned an impending earthquake in California in the early seventies that never came to pass, yet he was revered by COG members as "God's prophet and King." Later revelations of sexual relations with his own daughters and other cult members only caused Berg to use his letters to defend his practices.[10]

The Church of Bible Understanding, originally known as the Forever Family, is an example of a Bible-based cult. Founded in 1971 in Allentown, Pennsylvania, and headed by Stewart Traill, this religious group uses orthodox Christian terminology loaded with very unorthodox meanings. Cult observers Una McManus and John Cooper state that Traill's "understanding" of the Bible and its concealed meanings ("figures") are accepted as authoritative for cult members. They note that the group has "declared war on the powers of this world, including government, police, schools, parents, and churches."[11]

The Church of Armageddon, also known as the Love Family, looks to the vision of its members, including founder Paul Erdmann (also known as "Love Israel"), as its divine authority. Members renounce all worldly traditions of matrimony and are considered to be married to one another.[12]

In each of these examples, the words, visions or writings of a human leader are made equal to the Bible. In some cases they are looked upon as being of even greater authority than Scripture itself. Whenever someone claims to have a new revelation from God, he or she is making the same claim Muhammad made for the Koran and Joseph Smith made for *The Book of Mormon*.

2. *Presumptuous Leadership*

Not every cult leader is dangerous, but every one is presumptuous. Cult leaders think they alone have God's ultimate message for mankind. Therefore, in their minds, it becomes an absolute necessity that they deliver God's message at all costs and eliminate whatever opposition they face in doing so. Branch Davidian cult leader David Koresh's demand that his 58-minute "message to the world" be aired on radio in Waco, Texas, is typical of such a mind-set.

Early descriptions of David Koresh's and Jim Jones' backgrounds show striking similarities: broken homes, parental neglect, desire for power and control, excessive sexual appetites and the constant demand for loyalty and allegiance from their followers. Jim Jones and David Koresh may be extreme examples of dictatorial cult leaders, but they are not that far removed from the excessive behaviors of Sun Myung Moon, who dictates the marriages to total strangers of thousands of his followers, or David Berg, who authorized incest within the Children of God. Like this statement from the egotistical Reverend Ike, who said, "You can't lose with the stuff I use," the blasphemous and extravagant claims of deluded cult leaders are incredible. Here are just a few:

> *Judge Rutherford* (Jehovah's Witnesses): "Jesus Christ has returned to earth A.D. 1914 to establish the Theocratic Millennial Kingdom" (*The Kingdom,* 1933). The world is still awaiting this revelation.

> *Mary Baker Eddy* (Christian Science): "Death is an illusion" (*Science and Health,* 584:9). She succumbed to that illusion on December 3, 1910.

> *Father Divine* (Peace Mission): "I am God Almighty... the Holy Spirit personified... the Prince of Peace" (*New*

Day, July 16, 1949). "God" (George Baker, alias Father Divine) died in 1965.

Elijah Muhammad (Black Muslims): "Wallace Farad [Muslim version of Father Divine] is God himself! He is the one we have been looking for the last 2,000 years" (*New York Herald Tribune,* April 3, 1963). Wallace Farad (alias Allah) disappeared in 1934 and was never seen again.

Elizabeth Clare Prophet (Church Universal and Triumphant): "I am that I am" (*Teachings on the Path of Enlightenment*). She claims to be the channel of the "Great White Brotherhood" of "Ascended Masters." She and her followers are awaiting the end of the world in Montana.

Meher Baba (Sufism Reoriented): "I am Jesus Christ personified" (*Parvardigar*). Baba died on January 31, 1969.

Sun Myung Moon (Unification Church): "Jesus Christ will return by being born in the flesh in Korea as Lord of the Second Advent and True Parent of the world family" (*Divine Principle,* pp. 501ff.). Moon considers himself to be the Messiah incarnate.

David Berg (Children of God): "Forget not thy King.... Forsake not His ways, for he hath the key, even the Key of David! Therefore, thou shalt kiss the mouth of David. For thou art enamored of my words and thou art in love with me, thy Savior!" (*The Kingdom: A Prophecy,* August 20, 1971, Lo. No. 94). Berg is revered as King, Father, and David by his followers.

John Robert Stevens (The Walk): "We are going to turn and become the savior of the church" (*Living Word,* July 6, 1975). Stevens' followers denounce all churches but their own as the "harlot of Babylon."

Herbert W. Armstrong (Worldwide Church of God): "We grow spiritually more and more like God, until at the time of the resurrection—we shall then be born of God—we shall then be God" (*The U.S. and British Commonwealth*, p. 9).

David Koresh (Branch Davidians): "I am the Lamb of God" (*People*, March 15, 1993, p. 41). He died April 19, 1993.

3. *Exclusive Salvation*

This one criteria separates cults from denominations. Various Christian denominations may differ on their methods of ordination, their mode of baptism or their form of church government, but they generally don't consign each other to hell because of those differences. Cults, on the other hand, are always convinced they are the only ones going to heaven. All others are lost, damned, heretical or have the mark of the beast!

Jehovah's Witnesses believe that the Church Age ended in 1914 with the return of Christ to earth. Therefore, they do not meet in churches, but in Kingdom Halls. They say that only Jehovah's faithful witnesses (the 144,000) know and believe the truth—all others are lost. They clearly teach that only faithful Jehovah's Witnesses (both the "remnant" and the "other sheep") will survive the battle of Armageddon and see the salvation of Jehovah.[13]

Mormons believe they alone are the "latter-day saints" of God. Brigham Young said, "Every spirit that does not confess that God has sent Joseph Smith, and revealed the everlasting gospel to and through him, is of antichrist."[14] Speaking of non-Mormon Christian churches, Mormon apostle Orson Pratt said, "They have nothing to do with Christ, neither has Christ anything to do with them, only to pour out upon them the plagues."[15]

Seventh-day Adventists believe that the third angel's message in Revelation 14 requires the observance of Saturday Sabbath-keeping in order to guarantee eternal life. They allow that some Christians may live and die in ignorance of the third angel's message, and thus be given another chance to receive it at a special resurrection. But all who refuse will suffer annihilation.[16]

Christian Science founder Mary Baker Eddy said, "A Christian Scientist requires my work *Science and Health* for his textbook . . . because it is the voice of truth to this age . . . uncontaminated by human hypotheses."[17] In the glossary of *Science and Health,* the true church is defined as "that institution which affords proof of the apprehension of spiritual ideas and the demonstration of divine science."[18] Since Christian Science views itself as unerring and divine, it presumes that all other churches are erroneous.

Spiritualism declares it is the "highest message of truth which we have as yet grown to grasp."[19] Sir Arthur Conan Doyle said, "Spiritualism is the greatest revelation the world has ever known."[20] But Spiritualism (or spiritism), with its emphasis on communicating with departed spirits, has always opposed every major doctrine of Christianity (inspiration of the Bible, deity of Christ, the virgin birth, the atonement, and the resurrection) as anathema. Lord Dowling, a strong spiritualist advocate, said, "The doctrine of the Trinity seems to have no adherent in advance circles of the spirit world."[21]

Swedenborgians believe that Christ returned in the eighteenth century when their founder received what they claim to be the key to the interpretation of Scripture. They also believe Christ designated them alone to be the "New Jerusalem."[22] Following the highly speculative ideas of Emanuel Swedenborg, this small but influential cult claims to be the church signified by the New Jerusalem of the apocalypse. The rest of professing Christianity is viewed as "perverted from the truth."[23]

The Worldwide Church of God, under Herbert W. Armstrong and Garner Ted Armstrong, denounced all trinitarians as false prophets. They denounce all other churches as preaching a false gospel and a false Christ. They accuse others of "stupendous errors," "false conceptions," and "spiritual blindness."[24] Today, under the leadership of Joseph Tkach, the Worldwide Church of God has repudiated the Armstrong view.

The Unification Church (Moonies) teaches that Sun Myung Moon is the second messiah ("Lord of the Second Advent") sent to complete the work of salvation begun by Jesus Christ. Moon says of himself and his church, "No heroes in the past, no saints or holy men in the past, like Jesus or Confucius have excelled us."[25] Emphasizing his church exclusively, Moon claims, "We are the only people who truly understand the heart of Jesus, and the hope of Jesus."[26]

Once the process of spiritual deception reaches the point where the cultists believe they alone are God's people, then it follows logically that whatever they believe must be God's truth. By contrast, then, all who disagree with them are viewed as lost or deceived. Their belief that they have an exclusive corner on truth leads them to think they also have an exclusive corner on salvation.

4. *Limited Eschatology*

It was this "we are right; all others are wrong" mentality that enabled the followers of David Koresh to surrender their wives and daughters to him for sexual purposes. It also opened the door for them to contradict the clear teaching of Jesus against self-retaliation and take up arms to kill people in the name of God. It was this same mentality that provoked Muslim extremists from the Al-Salam Mosque in Jersey City, New Jersey, to bomb the World Trade Center in the name of God.

Christian-based cults have often begun as a result of some prophetic date-setting scheme. In most cases these eschatological prognosticators were sincere in their belief that Christ would soon return. However, when things did not work out the way they expected, they soon devised other explanations for their foiled mistakes.

In 1870, Charles T. Russell became influenced by Adventist teacher Jonas Wendell in Pittsburgh, Pennsylvania. Sparked with a renewed interest in the second coming of Christ, Russell organized a Bible class, began teaching and started publishing a magazine called *Zion's Watchtower and Herald of Christ's Presence.* By 1881, Russell incorporated Zion's Watchtower Tract Society. By 1886, he began publishing a seven-volume series entitled *Millennial Dawn,* later called *Studies in the Scriptures.*

Following the ideas of N.H. Barbour, Russell initially taught that Christ would return spiritually, not physically, in 1874 and finish the end-time harvest by 1914, the dawn of the millennial age. By correlating historical events with the length of the corridors in the Great Pyramid of Egypt, Russell confirmed his 1874 date for the beginning of the tribulation. Modern Jehovah's Witnesses reject Russell's calculation in favor of 1914. Cult expert Ronald Enroth observes, "To accommodate the change, a new edition of Russell's *Studies* (1923) simply added forty-one inches to the corridor's length in order to locate the starting point for the final years of earth's existence in 1914."[27]

Since there was no visible appearance of Christ in 1914, Jehovah's Witnesses believe He revealed Himself only to His faithful witnesses (the 144,000). Initially, Jehovah's Witnesses emphasized that when that number was complete (presumably around 1918), Christ would reveal to the world that He was already here. Today, they teach that there are two classes of followers: 1) The "congregation of God," the true church of Jehovah, and 2) the "great crowd" or "other sheep." The first group is limited to the 144,000 and will live in heaven, while the latter group is larger and will live on earth after Armageddon.[28]

Jehovah's Witnesses teach that they are the 144,000 "associate kings" who will rule with Christ in the millennium. They believe they are the only ones who know the truth that Christ returned on October 1, 1914, and ended the Church Age and the rule of nations. Hence, they recognize no church but their own and will not salute the flag of any nation. They also believe they alone will survive the battle of Armageddon and enter the millennium as God's true people.

Mormons also believe they hold a special place at the time of Christ's return. Calling themselves the Latter-day Saints, Mormons believe the time of the end is at hand and will culminate in the regathering of Israel in Jerusalem, the regathering of Ephraim (Mormons) at Zion (Independence, Missouri), and the regathering of the ten lost tribes to Zion. Mormons believe they will build the Temple of God in North America and recapture Zion from the Reorganized Church of Latter-day Saints (who hold title to the temple property in Independence after a split from the group that went on to Salt Lake City).

Mormons also believe they will be regathered first since Joseph Smith was a "pure Ephraimite," and the Ephraimites (Mormons) now hold the priesthood, having received the "fullness of the everlasting gospel" in these last days. They also believe that only faithful Mormons will enter the celestial kingdom (God's highest eternal order) and live eternally with their wives and children and continue to procreate more children in that celestial state. In other words, Mormons believe they hold center stage in God's eschatological program.

Moonies believe that all humanity will literally be saved by Sun Myung Moon, "Lord of the Second Advent." Even departed Christians will return to earth and serve the new messiah in the "True Family" of eternity. "Everybody who ever lived," notes Jack

Sparks in *The Mind Benders,* "good, bad, and indifferent—will participate in that great unified family formed around Moon, his wife and his children." Sparks then adds, "What malarkey! This is one of the most amazing schemes a human being has ever devised to deceive people and to bring them under oppressive domination."[29]

Notice again how one lie leads to another: We alone have the truth; we know what is best for you; we alone are the people of God; we alone will be in heaven. It is this kind of logic that sets up the ultimate conclusion: *All who are against us are against God.* Once the cultist is thus deceived, he or she becomes willing to do almost anything to protect the group from the enemy.

5. *Persecution Complex*

One does not have to look far to find plenty of examples of the cultic-persecution complex. David Koresh carried a Glock 9mm pistol and kept an arsenal of deadly weapons at his disposal because he believed the "agents of Satan" were about to attack him and launch the final battle of Armageddon.[30] Expecting a soon-to-come apocalypse, Koresh's Branch Davidians fortified their Mount Carmel complex outside Waco, Texas, to prepare for the end of the world.

Sheik Oman Abdel-Rahman told his Muslim followers to "kill the enemies of God in every spot to rid it of the descendants of apes and pigs fed at the tables of zionism, communism and imperialism."[31] Like a true cult leader, Abdel-Rahman assumes that his enemies are God's enemies as well.

There is little difference in the attitude of many of the more traditional or institutionalized cults. Down deep, they know they are different or out of step with traditional beliefs, so they expect to be rejected. Think of the abuse and rejection Mormons and Jehovah's Witnesses must experience as they go door to door to peddle their beliefs. "Jesus warned us that we would be perse-cuted," they say, almost inviting more persecution.

Institutionalized cults may have been started by fanatics, but as they grew, their leadership diversified and with time came to develop theological explanations for why they are persecuted. But in today's extremist cults, where the leader has a small but radical following, any rejection of the leader may result in direct hostility.

A nomadic cult founded by Jimmie T. Roberts of Kentucky has no name and wanders from place to place, often eating out of garbage cans. Nicknamed "the garbage eaters," they have left in their wake a trail of broken homes, battered women and abused children.[32] Believing that children are too young to know God, they assume little ones are "ruled by Satan." This mentality then assumes that unruly children are agents of the devil and need to have the devil beaten out of them.

Jim Jones was so paranoid because of his sinful lifestyle and unlawful activities that he knew intuitively he was in trouble. So he devised a scheme of moving around the country to avoid police investigators. Finally, when he wanted to avoid the federal gov-ernment, he moved his flock to Guyana. There in the sticky South American jungle, he armed his men with guns, laced everyone's Kool-Aid with cyanide, and prepared for an inevitable con-frontation with the outside world—a confrontation that cost the lives of more than 900 people.

Spiritual deception is a gradual, subtle process. Satan, the great deceiver, convinces the cult leader that he has found the truth no one else has ever discovered. Armed with this egotistical ammunition, the cultist begins to weave a web of religious decep-tion. He first falls victim to it himself, then he convinces others that he is right and manipulates their resources to further spread his message. In time, this leads to oppressive organizational con-trols to ensure this process continues.

God is against *false prophets* whose spiritual delusion causes them to invent their own message apart from God's truth. The Bible presents them in seven categories:

> *Self-deceived.* Some false teachers may be sincere, but they are still wrong. They have deceived themselves into believing their messages are true. As Jeremiah points out, their messages come psychologically from within their own minds and are not from God.

> *Liars.* Some false prophets are deliberate liars who have no intention of telling the truth. The apostle John says, "Who is the liar? It is the man who denies that Jesus is the Christ. Such a man is the antichrist—he denies the Father and the Son" (1 John 2:22).

> *Heretics.* These are people who preach heresy (false doctrine) and divide the church. Of them John said, "They went out from us, but they did not really belong to us" (1 John 2:19). The apostle Peter said, "There will be false teachers among you. They will secretly introduce destructive heresies....These men blaspheme in matters they do not understand" (2 Peter 2:1,12).

> *Scoffers.* There are some who do not necessarily promote false teaching so much as they outright reject the truth of God. Of them the Bible warns, "In the last days scoffers will come, scoffing and following their own evil desires" (2 Peter 3:3). The apostle Paul calls them "lovers of themselves...boastful, proud...conceited" (2 Timothy 3:2,4). Jude calls them "grumblers and faultfinders" (verse 16).

> *Blasphemers.* Those who speak evil of God, Christ, the Holy Spirit, the people of God, the kingdom of God, and the attributes of God are called blasphemers. Jude calls them godless men [who] "speak abusively against whatever they do not understand....They are clouds without rain... trees, without fruit...wild waves of the sea...wandering

stars" (Jude 10,12,13). The apostle Paul says that he himself was a blasphemer before his conversion to Christ (1 Timothy 1:13).

Seducers. Jesus warned that some false prophets will appear with miraculous signs and wonders to seduce or deceive the very elect "if that were possible" (Mark 13:22). Our Lord's implication is that spiritual seduction is a very real threat even to believers. This would account for the fact that a few genuine, but deceived, believers may be found among the cults.

Reprobates. This term means "disapproved," "depraved," or "rejected." Paul refers to those who have rejected the truth of God and turned to spiritual darkness. Consequently, God has given them over to a "reprobate mind" (Romans 1:28 KJV). They have so deliberately rejected God that they have become "filled with every kind of wickedness" (verse 29). As a result, they are "God-haters" (verse 30), whose behavior is "senseless, faithless, heartless, ruthless" (verse 31). These people are so far gone spiritually that they know it and don't care!

In Jesus' own prophetic message, the Olivet Discourse (Matthew 24–25), He warned, "Watch out that no one deceives you....Many will turn away from the faith...and many false prophets will appear and deceive many people....False Christs and false prophets will appear and perform great signs and miracles" (Matthew 24:4,10,11,24). Our Lord warned His disciples—and us—of the possibility of spiritual seduction by false prophets and teachers, especially as the end of the age approaches.

Only God
Can Prophesy!

Jesus Christ is the source of Bible prophecy and the subject of the prophetic Scriptures. The most dramatic prophecies in all the Bible point to the coming Messiah-Savior who would both suffer and reign. These ancient prophecies were so precisely fulfilled that there can be no serious doubt that they point to only one person who has ever lived—Jesus of Nazareth.

After His resurrection, Jesus told His disciples, "Everything must be fulfilled that is written about me in the Law of Moses, the Prophets, and the Psalms" (Luke 24:44). Christ Himself then taught the disciples which Old Testament Scriptures predicted His life and ministry. Luke 24:45 says, "Then opened he their minds so they could understand the Scriptures."

The New Testament writers were instructed by the Lord Himself regarding biblical prophecies and their fulfillment. The three-fold designation—law, prophets and psalms—refers to the three major divisions of the Hebrew Bible. Jesus was specifically stating that the entire Old Testament (law, prophets, psalms) was predicting His life, ministry, death and resurrection. Therefore, the preaching of the early Christian disciples was filled with references to Old Testament prophecies and their fulfillment in the person of Jesus Christ (see Acts 2:25-36; 3:22-23; 4:25-26; 13:46-49).

During His earthly ministry, Jesus was recognized as a "prophet" of God (Matthew 21:11; Luke 7:16) and a "teacher" from God (John 3:2). Jesus even referred to Himself as a "prophet" (Matthew 13:57; Luke 13:33). The early preaching of the apostles also emphasized the prophetic nature of Christ's ministry (Acts 3:24-26; 7:37). Matthew's gospel alone makes 65 references to Old Testament Scriptures, emphasizing their fulfillment in Christ.

Hobart Freeman has observed that, "messianic prophecy, in a real sense, may be regarded as the New Testament in the Old. Messianic prophecy is that which predicts the fulfillment of redemption and the establishment of the Kingdom of God through the Messiah."[1] Freeman points out that the Hebrew term "messiah" comes from the word *mashiach*, meaning to "anoint" for consecration and service. In Psalm 2, the Messiah ("Anointed One") is pictured as both the King of Israel and God's Son. This passage confirms the association of Jesus in the New Testament with the Messiah in the Old Testament. The fact that Jesus is called the Christ (Greek, *christos*, "anointed") is the new Testament equivalent of the Hebrew *mashiach*. He is Jesus the Christ—the Messiah.

The Prophet and the Prophetic Ministry

The prophetical histories are followed in the Hebrew canon by the prophetical books of prediction. The two form a unit in the middle portion of the threefold canon, under the common term "prophets." They are distinguished as the "former prophets" and "latter prophets." Leon Wood states: "The manner of speaking by the prophets may be best characterized as preaching."[2] Their messages also included symbolic actions (2 Kings 13:17-19), object lessons (Jeremiah 1:11-14), and written sermons (Jeremiah 36:4).

The Hebrew prophets were men of God who preached God's Word and also predicted the future. Their preaching had its roots in history since they preached to the people of their own generation. But their messages were also focused on the future and revealed events that were yet to come. In this regard the message of the prophets is supernatural, not natural. H.L. Ellison writes: "It is derived neither from observation nor intellectual thought, but from admission to the council chamber of God, from knowing God and speaking with Him."[3]

The revelation of God to the prophet is a process by which God reveals His secrets to the prophet (Amos 3:7). The term "reveal" (Hebrew, *galah*) means to "uncover," as in "uncovering the ear" (1 Samuel 9:15). Thus, when God "uncovers" the prophet's ear, He reveals what has been previously hidden (2 Samuel 7:27) so that the prophet "perceives" what the Lord has said (Jeremiah 23:18).

It is obvious, therefore, that the "Spirit of God" is necessary for prophetic inspiration (Isaiah 30). Thus, it was by the Spirit that the Word of the Lord was communicated to the prophet and by the Spirit that the Word was mediated to the people. This communion with God was indispensable to the prophetic consciousness as a medium of revelation, so that under the guidance of the Holy Spirit prophecy can sometimes be quite startling in the individuality and definiteness of its prediction of even remote events. So we see the full picture of prophecy as both a forthtelling of God's messages and a foretelling of God's actions. Through this means God continued to energize the prophet to speak for Him. Isaiah was such a man, addressing himself to his own times as he brought God's direction to the kings of Judah, and also a man seeing far into the future of God's plans for His people.

The Messiah in Prophecy

The high aspirations of the Old Testament writers and their ascriptions of God-like characteristics to a coming Prince, the Messiah, the son of David, compel the reader to see one who is more than a mere man. He was called both the son of David and the son of God. R.B. Girdlestone has pointed out that there is no definite statement that all these references in the Old Testament are to be fulfilled in one person, but such is the natural conclusion at which the recipients of the Old Testament arrived.[4] Yet, with the development of this messianic expectation came the frustrating close of the Old Testament canon, still awaiting the reality of these hopes embodied in that one man.

The New Testament based its entire apologetic on the fact that Jesus was the Messiah of the Old Testament, and that these were definite predictions which were conclusively fulfilled in this life. Jesus Himself was always aware of the "limitations" prophecy made on Him, since those prophecies "must be fulfilled." He subjected Himself completely to the course that they had, under God's direction, prescribed to Him, and considered the details of His life and death as something that must take place because it was written in the Word of God. At the same time, He saw Himself as the culminating point to which the whole of prophecy pointed.

The purpose of messianic prophecy was to make the Messiah known after He had fulfilled the event foretold. It served as a preparatory device to signal His arrival. How that "fulfillment" is recognized has been the source of ominous discussion. J.A. Alexander warns that although a doublesense of fulfillment is not impossible, it is unreasonable to assume it when any other explanation is admissible. He maintains that it is unlikely that both a common, natural event and a supernatural one would be couched in the same passage.[5]

We must be careful not to look for a fulfillment where none is intended or needed to complete the thought of the passage. Prophetic fulfillment is the consummation of a given prediction in history. The New Testament provides the best guideline to determining whether or not a certain event is fulfilled. It tells us where the prophets spoke of Christ. The indication we are given by the New Testament is that the Old Testament messianic references are a whole that refer totally to one Person—Jesus of Nazareth.

The Predictive Nature of Messianic Prophecy

It is difficult to consider the concept of messianic prophecy without assuming some type of "prediction" involved. In this discussion the word predict has been used in the ordinary sense of "foretell." The use of the Greek prefix *pro* indicates both "for" and "before." The prophet tells "for" God, and he tells "before" events will happen. This usage is certified by the parallel synonymy given to "foretell" and "foresee" in the New Testament. Peter, in Acts 2:30ff, speaks of David as a "prophet" because of his "foreseeing" (*proidon*) the resurrection of Christ. It would be ridiculous to insist that this be translated "forthseeing." We can see, then, that the prophets were not always restricted to a "local" or immediate fulfillment, but foresee the ultimate fulfillment in view.

Robert Culver gives two essential characteristics of predictive prophecy: it must predict the future as only God could know it and bring it to pass, and it must contain a degree of obscurity.[6] This quality of obscurity necessitates a direct fulfillment. It is only when the prophecy has become history that one may reflect upon it to realize that it has been fulfilled. Seen dimly at first, the intent of the prophecy becomes clear with its fulfillment. The New Testament recognizes the value of predictive prophecy and its fulfillment in using it as apologetical evidence to prove the supernaturalness and credibility of Christianity.

The Central Message of the Old Testament

Willis Beecher pointed out in the Stone Lectures at Princeton Theological Seminary that the messianic prophecies are not merely a "scarlet thread" that runs indiscernibly throughout the Old Testament, but that they are "everywhere the principal thing, that which underlies all the history, all the poetry, all the prophetic preaching, all the national worship, all the sayings of wisdom."[7] The whole Old Testament is the record of God's promises, and the New Testament is the record of their fulfillment.

After healing the lame man, the apostle Peter addressed the crowd who had witnessed the miracle and told them he had done this in the name and power of Jesus Christ, which God "had foretold through all the prophets" (Acts 3:18). Then Peter called upon them: "Repent, then, and turn to God, so that your sins may be wiped out" (3:19).

Edward J. Young observes: "According to Peter, the prophets spoke of the sufferings of Christ. These prophecies have been fulfilled, he reasons, and since they have been fulfilled, men should repent of their sins. Here in Israel was a phenomenon which could find no equal or parallel anywhere else in all the world. Here were men, raised up of God.... Here God did intervene in human history in a peculiar way."[8]

When the early Christians began to preach, they declared that Jesus of Nazareth was the promised Messiah of the Old Testament prophecies. Dr. Culver observes: "The New Testament record reports that they never failed to support these remarkable claims with proof that the claims were true."[9] They insisted that Jesus was the Christ on the basis of three essential arguments:

1. Jesus' resurrection

2. Their eyewitness account of what happened

3. Fulfillment of Old Testament prophecy

Within weeks of the resurrection, the early Christians were proclaiming the events in Jesus' life as fulfillment of specific prophecies. In the first Christian sermon, Peter announced: "This is what was spoken by the prophet Joel...David said about him...[that] he would raise up Christ to sit on his throne; seeing what was ahead, he spoke of the resurrection of Christ" (Acts 2:16,25,30).

This is the New Testament proof of the truthfulness of Christianity. The same approach is taken repeatedly in the New Testament. In following this line of proof the apostles were doing what had been done by God's prophets for centuries. They were pointing to the fulfillment of prophecy as the ultimate proof of the truthfulness of God's Word. In so doing, they were urging their listeners to believe the whole message of the gospel of Jesus Christ.

Old Testament Prophecies Fulfilled in the Life of Christ

The Old Testament is filled with prophecies about the human race, the nation of Israel and future events in general. But the most important prophecies are those that point to the coming of Christ. These are not merely isolated "proof texts." The whole of the Old Testament points the way to a coming future Messiah.

The laws of the Old Testament established the divine principle of righteousness. The history of Israel shows how God was preparing His people for the coming of the Messiah and how desperately they needed a Savior. The institutions of Old Testament religion (temple, priests, sacrifices) pointed to a coming One who would fulfill the reality of these symbols. The psalms were not only expressions of worship and praise, but prophecies of the coming Messiah. The prophetical books were collections of the sermons of the prophets and their predictions of the coming Messiah and the Messianic Age. Many of these predictions were recognized as messianic by the Jews, even before the time of Jesus. Here are ten examples:

Prophecy	*Subject*	*Fulfillment*
Genesis 3:15 "her offspring"	Seed of a woman	Galatians 4:4 "born of a woman"
Genesis 12:3 "all will be blessed through you"	Descendant of Abraham	Matthew 1:1 "the son of Abraham"
Genesis 49:10 "the sceptre will not depart from Judah"	Tribe of Judah	Luke 3:33 "the son of Judah"
Isaiah 9:6-7 "He will reign on David's throne"	Heir of David	Luke 1:32 "the throne of his father David
Micah 5:2 Bethlehem...will come...Ruler over Israel	Born in Bethlehem	Luke 2:4-7 "went to Bethlehem ...she gave birth"
Isaiah 7:14 "The virgin will be with child"	Born of a Virgin	Matthew 1:23 "The virgin will be with child...'God with us'"
Psalm 2:7 "You are my Son"	Declared the Son of God	Matthew 3:17 "This is my Son"
Isaiah 53:3 "He was despised and rejected"	Rejected by his own	John 1:11 "his own did not receive him"
Psalm 41:9 "my close friend... against me"	Betrayed by a friend	Matthew 26:50 "Friend, do what you came for"
Zechariah 12:10 "the one they have pierced"	Death by Crucifixion	Matthew 27:23 "Crucify him!"

There are about three hundred (300) distinct prophecies of Christ in the Old Testament. They are like pieces of a puzzle. Each presents a distinct element of the Savior's life and ministry, but the whole picture they portray can only be seen after their fulfillment. They remained obscure until Jesus came and put them all in clear relation to one another. The chances of all these prophecies being fulfilled in the life of one man is one chance in 84 followed by 131 zeroes.

These prophecies of Christ are overwhelming evidence of the divine origin of Scripture, the Messiahship of Jesus and the truth of Christianity. When viewed as a whole, the collective impact of these prophecies and their fulfillment in the Gospels cannot be easily dismissed. Dr. Culver states: "Any one of these alone might be explained away to the satisfaction of antagonistic people, but taken together their force is devastating to unbelief."[10]

What About Future Prophecies?

The accuracy of the fulfillment of the prophecies of Christ's first coming point to the certainty of the fulfillment of the prophecies of His second coming. John Phillips writes: "The prophecies relating to Christ's first coming have had a literal fulfillment, so we can confidently expect that the prophecies relating to His second coming will have an equally literal fulfillment."[11]

H.L. Ellison adds this important observation: "History shows us that there were only a few in Israel who had begun to take this revelation seriously by the time of our Lord, and there is no evidence that any of those had penetrated into its real meaning. There are elements in it that baffled men before Jesus of Nazareth made it luminous by fulfilling it. Even so today it baffles those who refuse to see Him as its fulfiller."[12]

While there is every reason to be convinced of the reality of future biblical prophecies, they can be accepted only by faith until the time of their fulfillment. But our faith in these prophecies is not based on some misplaced pious hope. It is based on the reality of past fulfilled prophecies of the Bible. These alone give us great confidence in the literal fulfillment of those future prophecies which must yet come to pass.

The exact nature of biblical prophecy and the specific and detailed manner of its fulfillment assure us that Christ will come again just as He said (John 14:1-3). We look forward to the unfolding of the future because we know that future is under the sovereign control of God.

John's gospel ends by reminding us that the "world could not contain" the books that should be written about Jesus Christ (John 21:25). But John himself, Jesus' personal disciple, states: "But these are written that ye might believe that Jesus is the Christ, the Son of God; and that believing ye might have life through his name" (John 20:31).

While biblical prophecies and their literal fulfillment may fascinate our curiosity and challenge our minds, they are ultimately intended to bring us to a personal point of decision and faith as well. If the Bible predicted these things would happen and they actually did happen, then we must take Jesus' claims seriously. If He alone fulfilled these prophecies, then He alone is the Savior— the Son of God. If not, He is a liar or a lunatic. But if so, then He is Lord of lords and King of kings. And if He is—He deserves our faith, our lives, and our complete devotion.

7

Can We Still Believe
in the Rapture?

"And so we can see there will be *no* rapture for the church!" the pastor thundered as he reached the end of his sermon. "All we can really look forward to is trouble, trouble, and more trouble!"

I sat bemused. It had been a classic defense of the amillennial position on the return of Christ. Like many amillennialists, the pastor, a dear friend, assumed that times of tribulation would continue throughout the Church Age and intensify toward the end times. Dismissing the idea of a pretribulational rapture (by which the church would escape the tribulation), he then dismissed the idea of any rapture at all, conveniently throwing 1 Thessalonians 4:13-18 right out the stained-glass windows!

Many who do not believe in a pretribulational rapture falsely assume there will be *no rapture at all*. This is a complete misconception. If one takes seriously passages like 1 Thessalonians 4:17, "We who are alive and remain shall be caught up together with them in the clouds, to meet the Lord in the air" (NASB), he or she is forced to conclude that there will be a rapture. The only real debate is over *when* it will occur.

Arguments raised against the rapture, on the basis that it is difficult to conceive of what it would be like for millions of people to suddenly disappear, are irrelevant. Joking remarks about bumping your head on the ceiling, or false teeth being left behind, or hundreds of car accidents suddenly occurring, are inconsequential in light of the fact that Scripture clearly states that we will be "caught up" (Greek, *harpazō*) into the air.

There will be a rapture! The only serious questions are: 1) When will it occur? and 2) What is its relationship to the return of Christ at the time of His second coming? If it can be proved that the body of believers (the church) will be "caught up" into heaven and that this "gathering together" (Greek, *episunagōgēs,* cf. 2 Thessalonians 2:1) is a separate event from the return of Christ in judgment, the pretribulationist has more than adequately made his case.

As John Feinberg has so convincingly demonstrated, one must first examine the basic passages about the rapture and the return and then look at secondary issues in light of the primary passages.[1] Pretribulationists merely need prove that the *dissimilarities* between the rapture passages and the return passages are significant enough to indicate that they are separate *events*.

The Nature of His Coming

The New Testament clearly teaches that Jesus Christ will "come again" (John 14:3 KJV) and "appear the second time" (Hebrews 9:28 KJV) for His own. He promised this to His disciples in the upper room. "I go to prepare a place for you," the Lord said, "and if I go and prepare a place for you, I will come again, and receive you unto myself; that where I am, there ye may be also" (John 14:2-3 KJV).

This is our Lord's first clear indication that He will return specifically and uniquely for His own. There is no reference in John 14 to a return in judgment upon the world. The promise of His return is specifically given to comfort the disciples during the time of His absence. Many believe this is the first clear reference in our Lord's teaching to the rapture of the believers.

In Hebrews 9:28, the writer also has believers in view when he states: "So Christ was once offered to bear the sins of many; and unto them that look for him shall he appear the second time without sin unto salvation" (KJV). Again, the promise of our Lord's return for His own is sounded loud and clear.

At least nine biblical terms are used in the New Testament to describe the return of Christ.

1. *Ho erchomenos.* "the coming one," as in Hebrews 10:37: "For yet a little while, and he that shall come will come" (KJV).

2. *Erchomai.* The act of coming. Used often of Christ's return (Matthew 24:30; John 14:3; 2 Thessalonians 1:10; Jude 14; Revelation 1:7; 22:20).

3. *Katabaino.* To "come down" or descend, as in 1 Thessalonians 4:16: "For the Lord himself shall descend from heaven with a shout" (KJV).

4. *Heko.* Result of one's coming, to have "arrived," as in Revelation 3:3: "I will come like a thief."

5. *Parousia.* Denotes arrival and presence (of a ruler) as in 1 Thessalonians 2:19: "For what is our hope, or joy, or crown of rejoicing? Are not even ye in the presence of our Lord Jesus Christ at his coming?"(KJV).

6. *Apokalupsis.* Meaning to "unveil" or "uncover." Rendered "appearing" (1 Peter 1:7 KJV) or "coming"

(1 Corinthians 1:7 KJV), or "revelation" (Revelation 1:1 KJV). Involves the unveiling of His divine glory.

7. *Phaneroo.* To "appear" (John 21:1 KJV), or be "manifested" (1 John 3:5 KJV): As in 1 John 3:2: "It doth not yet appear what we shall be. But we know that when he shall appear, we shall be like him; for we shall see him as he is" (KJV).

8. *Epiphaino.* To "appear" in full light or visibility. Denotes the "brightness" of His coming (2 Thessalonians 2:8 KJV) and the glory of "that day...unto all them that love his appearing" (2 Timothy 4:8).

9. *Horao.* To "see with the eyes," or to "appear" visibly, as in Hebrews 9:28: "and unto them that look for him shall he appear the second time" (KJV).

These terms are often used interchangeably to refer to the rapture or the return of Christ. One cannot build a convincing case for the distinction between the two events merely on the basis of the terms themselves.

The Time of His Coming

Most evangelicals agree as to the nature of Christ's coming, but there is substantial disagreement about the *time*. Millard Erickson observes: "The one eschatological doctrine on which orthodox theologians most agree is the second coming of Christ. It is indispensable to eschatology. It is the basis of the Christian's hope, the one event which will mark the beginning of the completion of God's plan."[2]

The New Testament picture of our Lord's return emphasizes at least six distinct aspects of the time of His coming. These may be summarized as follows:

1. *Future.* The entire emphasis of the New Testament points to a future return of Christ. He promised "I will come again" (John 14:3 KJV). The angels promised He would return (Acts 1:11). The apostles taught the certainty of His future return (Philippians 3:20; Titus 2:13; 2 Peter 3:3-8; 1 John 3:2-3).

2. *Imminent.* The return of Jesus Christ is always described as potentially imminent or "at hand" (Revelation 1:3, 22:10 KJV). Every generation of believers is warned to be ready for His coming, as Luke 12:40 states: "Be... ready also: for the Son of Man comes at an hour you think not" (KJV). Believers are constantly urged to look for the coming of the Lord (Philippians 3:20; Hebrews 9:28; Titus 2:13; 1 Thessalonians 5:6).

3. *Distant.* From God's perspective, Jesus is coming at any moment. But from the human perspective it has already been nearly 2000 years. Jesus hinted at this in the Olivet Discourse in the illustration of the man who traveled into a "far country" (heaven) and was gone "a long time" (Matthew 25:19). Peter also implies this in his prediction that men will begin to scoff at the second coming, after a long period of time (2 Peter 3:3-9).

4. *Undated.* While the rapture is the next major event on the prophetic calendar, it is undated, as is the glorious appearing of Christ. Jesus said: "But of that day and hour knoweth no man, no not the angels of heaven" (Matthew 24:36). Later he added: "It is not for you to know the times or the seasons" (Acts 1:7 KJV).

5. *Unexpected.* The mass of humanity will not be looking for Christ when He returns (Matthew 24:50; Luke 21:35). They will be saying "peace and safety," when suddenly caught unprepared by His return. So unexpected will His return be that "as a snare shall it come upon them that dwell on the face of the whole earth" (Luke 21:35 KJV).

6. *Sudden.* The Bible warns that Jesus will come "as a thief in the night... (and) then sudden destruction" will come upon the unbelieving world (1 Thessalonians 5:2-3 KJV). His return for the bride will occur in a flash: "in a moment, in the twinkling of an eye... for the trumpet shall sound, and the dead (believers) shall be raised incorruptible, and we (living believers) shall be changed" (1 Corinthians 15:52 KJV).

Two Aspects of His Coming

There are certain similarities between the rapture passages and the second coming passages, since they both refer to future events relating to our Lord's return. But *similarity* does not mean they are referring to the *same* event. Pretribulationists believe that there are enough substantial differences between the two aspects of Christ's coming so as to render them as two separate and distinct events.

The distinction between these two phases of the second coming is substantiated by the contrast between those passages that refer to our Lord's coming for His church and those referring to His coming to judge the unbelieving world. Thomas Ice has provided the following list to identify those distinctions.[3]

Rapture Passages	*Second Coming Passages*
John 14:1-3	Daniel 2:44-45
Romans 8:19	Daniel 7:9-14
1 Corinthians 1:7-8	Daniel 12:1-3
1 Corinthians 15:51-53	Zechariah 14:1-15
1 Corinthians 16:22	Matthew 13:41
Philippians 3:20-21	Matthew 24:15-31
Colossians 3:4	Matthew 26:64
1 Thessalonians 1:10	Mark 13:14-27

Rapture Passages	*Second Coming Passages*
1 Thessalonians 2:19	Mark 14:62
1 Thessalonians 4:13-18	Luke 21:25-28
1 Thessalonians 5:9	Acts 1:9-11
1 Thessalonians 5:23	Acts 3:19-21
2 Thessalonians 2:1	1 Thessalonians 3:13
1 Timothy 6:14	2 Thessalonians 1:6-10
2 Timothy 4:1	2 Thessalonians 2:8
Titus 2:13	2 Peter 3:1-14
Hebrews 9:28	Jude 14-15
James 5:7-9	Revelation 1:7
1 Peter 1:7,13	Revelation 19:11–20:6
1 John 2:28–3:2	Revelation 22:7,12,20
Revelation 3:10	

Ice comments that the rapture is characterized in the New Testament as a "translation coming," in which Christ comes for His church, taking her to His Father's house (John 14:3; 1 Thessalonians 4:15-17; 1 Corinthians 15:51-52).[4] Here, He claims her as His bride and the marriage supper of the Lamb begins. Whatever view one holds in regard to our Lord's return, one thing is clear in prophetic Scripture. The marriage occurs *in heaven* (Revelation 19:7-9) *before* the triumphal return of Christ with His redeemed church at His side (Revelation 19:11-16).

Non-pretribulationists are at a virtual loss to explain how the church got to heaven prior to returning with Christ at the battle of Armageddon. At best, some suggest they are "caught up" after the tribulation only to return immediately with the Lord.[5] This arrangement, however, leaves little or no time for the wedding!

The return of Christ is a series of events fulfilling all end-time prophecies. These include predictions of His coming *for* His church and His coming *with* His church. Pretribulationists divide the return of Christ in two main phases: the rapture of the church and the second coming of Christ. In the first aspect, our Lord comes to take His own (the living and the dead) to be with Him. In the second aspect, He returns with His resurrected and raptured saints to win the battle of Armageddon and to establish His kingdom on earth (Revelation 5:10, "and we shall reign on the earth").

The Bible is filled with detailed predictions about both aspects of Christ's return. Just as the Scripture predicted two aspects of our Lord's first coming (His suffering and His glory), so it predicts two aspects of His *second* coming. The different aspects of our Lord's return are clearly delineated in the Scripture. The only real issue in the eschatological debate is the time *interval* between them.

Pretribulationists place the seven-year tribulation period between the rapture and the return. This allows for the proper fulfillment of Daniel's "seventieth week," and it clearly separates the rapture from the return. Other views are covered in other chapters. It is my purpose merely to substantiate that there are adequate *dissimilarities* between the events of the rapture and events associated with the return.

Contrast Between the Rapture and the Return

Rapture	*Return*
1. Christ comes *for* His own (John 14:3; 1 Thessalonians 14:17; 2 Thessalonians 2:1).	1. Christ comes *with* His own (1 Thessalonians 3:13; Jude 14; Revelation 19:14).
2. He comes in the *air* (1 Thessalonians 4:17).	2. He comes to the *earth* (Zechariah 14:4; Acts 1:11).
3. He *claims* His bride (1 Thessalonians 4:16-17).	3. He comes *with* His bride (Revelation 19:6-14).
4. Removal of *believers* (1 Thessalonians 4:17).	4. Manifestation of *Christ* (Malachi 4:2).

Rapture	*Return*
5. *Only* His own see Him (1 Thessalonians 4:13-18).	5. *Every eye* shall see Him (Revelation 1:7).
6. *Tribulation* begins (2 Thessalonians 1:6-9).	6. Millennial *kingdom* begins (Revelation 20:1-7)
7. Saved are *delivered from wrath* (1 Thessalonians 1:10; 5-9)	7. Unsaved *experience the wrath of God* (Revelation 6:12-17).
8. *No signs* precede rapture (1 Thessalonians 5:1-3)	8. *Signs* precede second coming (Luke 21:11,15).
9. Focus: *Lord and church* (1 Thessalonians 4:13-18).	9. Focus: *Israel and kingdom* (Matthew 24:14).
10. *World* is deceived (2 Thessalonians 2:3-12).	10. *Satan* is bound (Revelation 20:1-2).

Is the Rapture in the Bible?

The church's hope is the rapture. She awaits the Savior who is coming for His bride. The church may endure persecution, trouble, and difficulty in the meantime. But she is not the object of divine wrath. The church does not await destruction as the world does. Rather, she awaits the coming of her Lord and King. Peter explains that the present world is "reserved for fire, being kept for the day of judgment and destruction of *ungodly* men" (2 Peter 3:7).

The church is pictured in Scripture as the wife of the Lamb (Revelation 19:7-9). She is not the object of the wrath of the Lamb. He does not beat her up and then marry her! Or marry her, then beat her up! He may discipline her in love. But His ultimate purpose is to present her to the Father as His perfect bride.

The rapture (or "translation") of the church is often paralleled to the "raptures" of Enoch (Genesis 5:24) and Elijah (2 Kings 2:12). In each case, the individual disappeared or was caught up into heaven. At His ascension, our Lord Himself was "taken up" into heaven (Acts 1:9 KJV). The biblical description of the rapture involves both the resurrection of deceased believers and the translation of living believers into the air to meet the Lord (1 Thessalonians 4:16-17; 1 Corinthians 15:51-52).

The concept of the rapture is expressed in the biblical terms "caught up" (Greek, *harpazō)* and "gathered together" (Greek, *episunagōgēs).* Hogg and Vine observe that *harpazō* is the same verb used of Paul ("whether in the body or apart from the body," 2 Corinthians 12:2-4); Philip ("spirit...caught away Philip," Acts 8:39 KJV); and the man child ("caught up to God," Revelation 12:5 KJV).[6] This explains that *harpazō* conveys the idea of force suddenly exercised and is best rendered "snatch" (John 10:28-29), where Jesus promises that no one can "snatch" (KJV) His own out of His hand. He alone does the "snatching" at the time of the rapture!

By contrast, *episunagōgēs* refers to that which results from the "catching up" *(harpazō).* Once caught up into the clouds, we shall be "gathered together" with the Lord. In commenting on 2 Thessalonians 2:1, Hogg and Vine observe: "Here it refers to the 'rapture' of the saints into the air to meet and to be forever with the Lord."[7] The basic meaning is to "assemble together." The raptured church is pictured as the great "assembly" (synagogue) in the sky. Milligan observes: "The word goes back to the saying of the Lord in Mark 13:27 ("gather His elect"), and is found elsewhere in the New Testament only in Hebrews 10:25, where it is applied to the ordinary religious assembling of believers as an anticipation of the great assembling at the Lord's coming."[8]

Of course there is a rapture! There can be no valid system of biblical eschatology without a rapture. The church will be "caught up" and "gathered together" with her Lord. The only real debate is over the question of when. Any eschatological system that dismisses the rapture as some hoax has forfeited the essential biblical teaching that Christ will come and snatch away His bride to the great assembly in heaven.

Amillennialists, postmillennialists, and posttribulationists alike must account for the rapture in their eschatological schemes. So away with all talk of debunking the very idea of the rapture. It is taught in these passages of Scripture as clearly as any other doctrine. And any legitimate eschatological system must account for it. There will be a rapture. The question is whether it is separate from the return of Christ or a part of the same event.

Are the Events of the Return Distinctly Different?

Those who reject a pretribulational rapture usually argue that the rapture happens simultaneous with the return of Christ.[9] The Lord descends from heaven, "catches up" the church, and then returns to set up His kingdom. In order to make the rapture occur simultaneous to the return, such systems emphasize the *similarities* between the two: In both Christ comes at the end of the age to bring in the consummation of all things.

However, a simple survey of the second coming passages reveals some significant differences. Unlike the rapture of the saints, several passages refer to our Lord's coming *with* His saints: 1 Thessalonians 3:13, "at the coming of our Lord Jesus Christ with all his saints" (KJV); Jude 14, "Behold, the Lord cometh with ten thousands of his saints" (KJV); Revelation 19:14, "and the armies which were with him in heaven followed him upon white horses, clothed in fine linen, white and clean" (KJV). Revelation 19:11-16 certainly refers to the church returning with Christ to judge the unbelieving world, overthrow the antichrist and the false prophet, and establish the millennial reign of Christ on earth.

Other second-coming passages refer to a series of events that find no reference at all in the rapture passages: returning to the earth, splitting the Mount of Olives (Zechariah 14:4); punishing the wicked in flaming fiery vengeance (2 Thessalonians 1:6-9); overthrowing political and ecclesiastical "Babylon" (Revelation 17–18); winning the battle of Armageddon (Revelation 16:16-21); defeating the antichrist and the false prophet (Revelation 19:19-21); binding Satan in the bottomless pit (Revelation 20:1-3); and establishing the reign of the saints upon the earth for 1,000 years (Revelation 20:4-10).

All of these events associated with the return of Christ are completely distinct from the promise to rapture and assemble the church in heaven. These distinctions are surely sufficient to warrant viewing them as separate, though related, events. Having established this distinction, pretribulationists have adequate ground for viewing these events as being separated by the tribulation period.

The church is promised that the coming of the Lord will result in her being "caught up" and "gathered together" unto Him. It is this promise of the rapture, not of the wrath, that is in view in Revelation 3:10, where the Scripture promises, "I will keep you *from* [Greek, *ek* 'out of'] the hour of trial that is going to come upon the whole world" (KJV). Only a pretribulational rapture makes this promise a reality.

Ten Reasons for a Pretribulational Rapture[10]

1. ***Christ promised to keep the church from the tribulation.*** In Revelation 3:10, the risen Christ said the church would be *kept from* (literally, "preserved," or "protected *out* of") the hour of trial, or divine retribution, that is coming on the whole world.

2. ***Tribulation judgments are the "wrath of the Lamb."*** Revelation 6:16 depicts the cataclysmic judgments of the end times as the wrath of Christ. Revelation 19:7-9 depicts the church as the bride of the Lamb. She is

not the object of His wrath, which is poured out on an unbelieving world.

3. *Jesus told His disciples to pray that they would escape the tribulation.* In Luke 21:36, He said: "Be always on the watch, and pray that you may be able to escape all that is about to happen." Remember, even Lot was given a chance to escape Sodom before divine judgment fell.

4. *His coming in the clouds means the church's deliverance has come.* Jesus told His disciples to "lift up your heads, because your redemption is drawing near" (Luke 21:28). The hope of the church is not in surviving the judgment of tribulation but in escaping it.

5. *God will call His ambassadors home before declaring war on the world.* In 2 Corinthians 5:20, believers are called "Christ's ambassadors," who appeal to the world to be reconciled to God before it is too late. In biblical times, one's ambassadors were recalled when it was time to make war with the enemy.

6. *Moral restraint will disappear when the church is taken home.* Second Thessalonians 2:1-11 warns that *after* the "coming of our Lord" and "our being gathered to Him," the "man of lawlessness" (antichrist) will emerge on the world scene. The church's restraining ministry of "salt" and "light" will no longer hold back the tide of evil.

7. *The rapture will happen in the "twinkling of an eye."* First Corinthians 15:51-52 promises that "in a flash, in the twinkling of an eye ... the dead shall be raised imperishable and we [living at the rapture] will be changed" (KJV). This instantaneous disappearance will terminate the church's early ministry.

8. *The rapture will take place in the air.* Unlike the glorious appearing, when Christ descends to earth, splits the Mount of Olives, overthrows the antichrist, and binds Satan, the rapture will occur when we are "caught

up together ... to meet the Lord in the air" (1 Thessalonians 4:17).

9. ***The woman who suffers persecution during the tribulation symbolizes Israel.*** This is a very important point. The woman who delivers the male child (Christ) represents the nation of Israel. Israel, not the church, brought forth Christ, and He in turn brought forth the church. He is the founder of the church, not its descendant. Therefore, the persecuted "saints" of the tribulation are Jewish: the remnant of the woman's seed (Revelation 12:1-2,5-6,17).

10. ***The marriage of Christ (the Lamb) and His bride (the church) takes place before the battle of Armageddon.*** The Bible describes the fall of "Babylon" (kingdom of antichrist) in Revelation 17–18. But *before* it tells of Christ's return to conquer the antichrist, it tells us "the wedding of the Lamb has come, and His bride has made herself ready" (Revelation 19:7-8). This clearly indicates the bride has been taken to heaven earlier, and that she returns with Christ and the host of the "armies of heaven ... dressed in fine linen, white and clean" (Revelation 19:8,14 KJV).

The New Testament clearly distinguishes *two separate future events:* the rapture of the church by Christ and the return of Christ with the church. It is not surprising that non-pretribulationists often ignore these biblical distinctions because they are at a loss to explain how such different events could all happen simultaneously as only one event. As we have seen, the rapture and the return are different in nature and therefore represent separate and distinct events.

The Blessed Hope

The Bible refers to Christ's return as the "blessed hope—the glorious appearing of our great God and Savior, Jesus Christ"

(Titus 2:13). The sheer joy of knowing that one day we will be raptured into the presence of Christ causes all earthly concerns to fade into oblivion. It is no wonder the Bible reminds us that "our citizenship is in heaven. And we eagerly await a Savior from there, the Lord Jesus Christ" (Philippians 3:20).

Dave Hunt notes that a person cannot look for the coming of Christ at any moment if he believes Jesus will not return until after the tribulation period. Hunt observes, "If the rapture could not occur until after the antichrist has first appeared, or until the end of the great tribulation, surely such language would not have been used.[11] He goes on to point out that the imminent return of Christ was the daily hope of the early Christians.

Rather than possessing an escapist mentality, prophecy students have an earnest desire to be ready at all times to meet the Lord, who could come at any moment to call us home. We want to be watching, ready, and serving. That's what our Lord commanded in the Olivet Discourse (see Matthew 24:42-46).

A readiness to meet the Lord when He returns is one of the great motivations of the Christian life. First, we must be certain that we know Christ as our Savior. Second, we must live out our faith by being ready to meet Him at any moment. Dave Hunt writes, "That is the Christian's hope. Heaven is our real home and that is where our hearts are—with Him."[12]

Living in the Light of Eternity

Each of us must plan our lives as though we will live for many more years to come. We have a responsibility to our families, our children, our grandchildren, and other people around us. But we must also live our lives as though Jesus could come at any moment. It is difficult for non-Christians to understand the balanced approach we must have toward the future. We Christians do not fear the future because we believe God controls it. But at the same time, we do not view it with unbridled optimism.

The tension between living for today and looking forward to tomorrow is one of the realities of life. Christians especially find themselves caught in that tension between the here and now and the hereafter. Though we are enjoying our daily walk of faith here on earth, we also have a desire to depart and be with Christ. The apostle Paul addressed this tension when he wrote, "For to me, to live is Christ and to die is gain" (Philippians 1:21).

Bible prophecy emphasizes that we need to be ready because Christ could come at any time. Because of the imminence of His return, we must be waiting and watching every moment. At the same time, we have serious responsibilities to fulfill in this world. We cannot use our belief in Christ's return as an excuse to avoid our responsibilities.

The Bible tells us not only how to prepare for the future but how to live right now. It tells us about the destiny of the nations, but it also speaks about our personal destiny. As the sands of time slip through the hourglass of eternity, we are all moving closer to an appointment with God in the future.

Living in the light of eternity helps us remember our real destiny. We are not limited by earthly events because we have a heavenly future. We have more living ahead of us than we do behind us—no matter what our age may be. Every believer in Jesus Christ can look forward to the rapture, the marriage supper, the triumphal return, the millennial kingdom and all eternity.

The Puritan pastor John Flavel once said: "Faith is casting your soul into the ocean of eternity on the hope of a promise."[13] That is exactly what everyone does who places his or her trust in Jesus Christ. We know that our future is secure because we know who holds our future. We live by faith today, knowing that tomorrow is in His hand.

8

What About Those
Who Are Left Behind?

The rapture of the church will remove the bride of Christ to heaven. Those left behind will face the difficult and dreadful times known in the Bible as the great tribulation (Revelation 7:14). This will be a time of terrible war, conflict, suffering and death. While it will be possible for some people to be saved during this time, it will generally cost them their lives.

The process of God's judgments upon the world are unleashed after the rapture by the opening of the seven seals (Revelation 6). These result in a series of catastrophic events that express the "wrath of the Lamb." Each opening of a seal hurtles the world further along a course of ultimate disaster. Eventually, the opening of the seventh seal (Revelation 8:1) results in the sounding of seven trumpets, which intensify the judgments even further.[1]

The trumpet judgments (Revelation 8-11) and the bowl judgments (Revelation 15-16) have several obvious similarities. Merrill Tenney has observed, "The seven bowls are a closely knit series

123

following each other in rapid succession. They parallel the trumpets in their spheres of action, but they are more intense."[2]

While there are some differences in the two accounts (wormwood, locusts, kings of the East, Armageddon), there are far more similarities. Both accounts describe a succession of events that result from catastrophic wars:

1. Vegetation destroyed

2. Sea waters polluted

3. Fresh waters polluted

4. Air pollution

5. Demonic plagues

6. Armies of millions

7. Final victory of God

One of the key interpretive issues in the book of Revelation has to do with the issues of divine sovereignty and human agency. In other words, who is doing what? Are these judgments directly from the hand of God (cosmic destruction)? Or are they the result of human conflict (nuclear war)? While it is easy to speculate one way or another, we must let the text of Scripture speak for itself.

The seal judgments (Revelation 6) result when Christ Himself breaks the seven seals. Yet, those involve people killing one another (6:4-8). They also involve geological forces such as earthquakes (6:12) and cosmic forces such as the sun, moon, stars, and heavens (6:12-14). The trumpet judgments result from angelic pronouncements (8:7) and include cosmic and geological forces (8:7-12). They also seem to include demonic forces (locusts from the bottomless pit) and human armies and modern weapons (9:16-19). The bowl judgments follow the same pattern and include the same elements.

All of these judgments in Revelation (seals, trumpets, bowls) include divine, demonic, human, and natural forces. Satan is pictured as spewing out his wrath on the earth (12:12). The beast and the false prophet are pictured as his human agents (13:1-18; 19:19-21). At times the forces of evil are an individual (beast or antichrist). At times they are an entire system of human government (Babylon). In other passages, the evil forces seem to be coming from hell itself (9:1-11). But time and time again our attention is refocused on the immediate factor: human armies bent on mass destruction. Thus we read of swords, weapons, armies, horsemen, flamethrowers, kings, battles and Armageddon.

The grand overview of the apocalypse presents every possible perspective on the catastrophic destruction that will come in the future. Nothing in previous human history compares to the intensity or extent of these disasters. The whole world is pictured as being at war, and the entire planet is about to be destroyed.

The overarching theology of the apocalypse touches every possible element of the coming conflict:

> Divine—God is in control of all forces.
>
> Satanic—Satan tries to destroy mankind.
>
> Demonic—Demons assist Satan's attempt.
>
> Angelic—Angels announce the judgments of God.
>
> Human—Armies are at war over the world.
>
> Geologic—The planet is reeling from destruction.
>
> Cosmic—The heavens are shaken and depart.

The World at War

The destruction described in the first four seals is a preview of what is to come in the trumpet and bowl judgments. First, we have the wide-angle panorama; then the detailed snapshots follow. The seer is describing a vision of worldwide destruction that shall come at some time in the future prior to the return of Christ.

The final seal is opened (Revelation 6:12-17) and the planet is shaken to its very core. Disorder reigns supreme; the powers of nature and human government collapse. Chaos ensues, and people call upon the rocks and mountains to "fall on us." In this awful moment of divine retribution, there is no repentance by the ungodly. They call upon the powers of nature to deliver them but they will not call upon God.

A "great earthquake" rocks the planet. The sun is darkened, the stars fall, and the heavens (atmosphere) depart "as a scroll." These passages clearly indicate some sort of nuclear or cosmic disaster which causes the entire planet to be shaken so that the sun, moon and stars appear to be moving and the atmosphere "departs as a scroll" (Revelation 6:14). John's description is very similar to that in 2 Peter 3:10. In both passages, the "heavens" refer to earth's atmosphere, not the dwelling place of God (which, of course, remains undamaged). But the planet is totally devastated, and universal terror reigns supreme in the hearts of unregenerate men.

What is all of this? Our text says it is the "wrath of the Lamb; for the great day of his wrath is come and who shall be able to stand?" (Revelation 6:16-17). Some limit the wrath to the sixth seal and onwards. Some divide the first four or five seals into the first half of the tribulation, and seal six initiates the last half, or the great tribulation. However, there is nothing in the text itself to indicate this. The reference to the "wrath of the Lamb" could just as easily be a summary statement covering His opening of all six seals.

The opening of each seal leads to a progression of events that intensifies the divine judgment ("wrath of the lamb"). That intensity culminates in international wars, planetary devastation, and what certainly sounds like the consequences of nuclear holocaust. Despite the human instruments who cause this devastation, the catastrophe itself is called the "great day of the Lord." Amos predicted it would be a day of darkness (Amos 5:18). Isaiah said it will "shake terribly the earth" (Isaiah 2:19,21 KJV) and make the earth empty and waste, turning it "upside down" and scattering the inhabitants of the earth (Isaiah 24:1).

With the opening of the first six seals, the process of judgment begins. The world is at war, and the future of the planet is in jeopardy. But behind the scenes, one thing remains clear: God is still in control. Jesus Christ is in charge of the opening of the seals, and the sovereign will of heaven prevails despite the inhumanity of a depraved and corrupt society.

A World Gone Mad

Since 1945, when the atomic bomb was dropped on Hiroshima, Japan, mankind has lived with the threat of nuclear annihilation. The "baby boomers"—those born in the population boom after World War II—could just as easily be called the generation of the bomb. Many psychologists believe that people in this generation do not think like any generation that has preceded them because they have to live with the reality of their own vulnerability every day.

Educator Arthur Levine has described the current mentality as "going first class on the Titanic." In his study sponsored by the Carnegie Foundation for the Advancement of Teaching, Levine found that today's students are self-centered, individualistic "escapists" who want little responsibility for solving society's problems, but who want society to provide them with the opportunity to fulfill their pleasures. They have given up noble causes because they have given up any real hope of solving the world's problems. They see themselves on a hopeless voyage destined for disaster. Unable to turn the ship around, they simply clamor for the first-class seats so they can enjoy the ride until the inevitable strikes.

It should not surprise us, therefore, that people today will spare almost no expense for elaborate vacations, expensive trips, and romantic cruises. They are trying to pretend everything is all right, even though they know it isn't.

While the desire for peace clings to the deepest crevice of the human heart, the prospects for global destruction are far greater than the prospects for global peace. Undoubtedly, men will continue to strive for peaceful solutions. But beyond the attempts at peace is the final holocaust.

The Final Blast

The Bible predicts the final devastation in "one hour" (Revelation 18:10) of the prophetic "Babylon," the symbolic name for the kingdom of the antichrist. The Bible says, "all your riches and splendor have vanished, never to be recovered" (Revelation 18:14). Even the merchants and sailors will not come near this land but will "stand far off, terrified at her torment," and crying out, "In one hour such great wealth has been brought to ruin!" (Revelation 18:15,17).

The apostle Peter provides an even more vivid description of the final blast that shall devastate this planet when he warns, "But the day of the Lord will come like a thief. The heavens will disappear with a roar; the elements will be destroyed by fire, and the earth and everything in it will be laid bare" (2 Peter 3:10).

John Phillips notes that Peter's prophecy of a great end-times conflagration of the earth and its atmosphere uses precise terminology that accurately describes a nuclear explosion. The *elements* (Greek, *stoicheia*) are defined by Liddell and Scott's *Lexicon* as "the components into which matter is divided" (or atoms), and the term *dissolved* (Greek, *luo*) comes from the basic Greek word meaning to "loose" that which is bound (as in nuclear fission). The term *great noise* (Greek, *rhoizedon*) is found nowhere else in the New Testament and signifies "a rushing sound as of roaring flames." The term *fervent heat* is derived from the Greek medical term *kausoo,* denoting a fever. But Peter's use of it in application to inanimate objects is the only such known usage anywhere in Greek literature. Thus, Phillips concludes, "Peter described in accurate terms the untying of the atom and the resulting rushing, fiery destruction which follows it.[3]

The Seven Trumpets

John's description of the trumpet judgments (Revelation 8:2–11:19) sounds very similar to a global holocaust. The entire planet will be affected by massive destruction, loss of life, and human suffering. The chaos that results will destabilize both the global economy and the world government predicted in Revelation 13.

The seventh seal of the scroll is finally opened in Revelation 8:1. The imagery that follows, including the half-hour of silence, follows the liturgy of the Jewish temple services.[4] After the sacrificial lamb was slain, the altar of incense was prepared. Two of the priests would go into the holy place and take the burnt coals and ashes from the golden altar and relight the lamps of the golden candlestick. One priest filled the golden censer with incense, while the other placed burning coals from the altar into a golden bowl. Deep silence fell over the temple during this solemn ceremony.

The picture here in Revelation is very similar. There is silence for one half-hour after the opening of the seventh seal. It is the silence of solemn worship. But it is also the holy hush before the ungodly storm—one last gasp before all hell breaks loose.

The angel offers the "prayers of the saints (believers)" from the golden censer (8:3). Then he fills the censer with fire from the altar and "cast[s] it into the earth" (8:5). This initiates the conflagration that is about to engulf the planet. Bruce Metzger writes, "Then—bang! Catastrophic consequences follow. Seven angels, one after another, blow their trumpets, announcing hail-storm with fire and blood descending, volcanic eruption, blood in the sea, blight in the land ... climaxed by an enormous plague of demonic locusts."[5]

These trumpets may be associated with nuclear or chemical warfare. The devastation that they predict was unknown and unfathomable in the ancient world. These destructions are certainly beyond anything known to the people of John's day, which makes the apocalypse all the more fascinating. There is no way John could have merely imagined these great catastrophes had he not seen them by divine permission in these visions. The cataclysmic destruction he pictures certainly sounds like the devastating effects of nuclear war.

A *limited nuclear exchange* between the modern superpowers would kill an estimated one billion people and seriously injure another 500 million. The immediate results would include:

- Radiation poisoning

- Environmental destruction

- Uncontrollable fires

- Massive food shortages

- Air and water pollution

- Soil contamination

- Unparalleled human suffering

Long-term results would mean the decivilization of the earth. Human culture would be thrown back into primitive survival tactics. Roving in bands of lawless raiders would become the only means of survival in contaminated areas. Whole populations would likely be wiped out in North America, Europe, or the Middle East. Africa, Australia, South America, and parts of Asia might be the only survivors left on the planet.

John the revelator paints a picture of global conflagration. He sees the vegetation burned up, a mountain of fire (fireball) falling into the sea, stars falling from heaven and the darkening of the sun by a thickened atmosphere. It is no wonder that he hears an angel flying through heaven shouting, "Woe, woe, woe, to the inhabiters of the earth" (Revelation 8:13).

The results of this destruction are so vast that one-third of all the trees and all the grass on the entire planet burn up. Such a massive destruction of vegetation would result in food shortages and a limited air supply. John provides no explanation of how this will occur. One gets the impression that he watched this destruction in utter amazement.

The very fact that the Bible predicts a massive global conflagration at the end of human history, coupled with the fact that we live in a time when such a catastrophe is humanly possible, ought to be a wake-up call to everyone on the planet!

John Phillips writes, "Truly the dawning of the atomic age is of great prophetic significance.... We have lived on the edge of a potential holocaust for so long we find it difficult to believe that we are on the brink of the Rapture of the Church and the subsequent unleashing of apocalyptical doom."[6] Ironically, even the seer's description of "hail and fire" fits the nuclear description of an explosion of fire and ice.

The first four trumpets resulted in human devastation brought about by war and the forces of nature. But the last three trumpets involve supernatural forces—angels and demons. These last three trumpets take us behind the scenes of the human conflict to see the ultimate spiritual warfare being fought for the control of the earth.

The extent of these judgments affects the whole world. If the church were still on earth during this time, she would be caught right in the middle of this great global disaster. Even non-dispensationalist Leon Morris admits, "The trumpet judgments do not concern the church as such. They are God's judgments on the world."[7] But if the church were still in the world, she could hardly escape such worldwide devastation. But there is no mention of the church in these chapters because she has already gone home to glory in the rapture.

Can Anyone Be Saved After the Rapture?

John Walvoord writes, "The question has often been asked, 'Will anyone be saved after the rapture?' The Scriptures clearly indicate that a great multitude of both Jews and Gentiles will trust in the Lord after the church is caught up to glory."[8] Later, two "witnesses" are introduced who are instrumental in the conversion of the Jews (Revelation 11:3-12).

Premillennialists believe Christ will return at the end of the Church Age and judge the world in order to set up His kingdom on earth for a literal 1,000 years. Most also believe there will be a great tribulation period on earth prior to the return of Christ. Among premillennialists are those who believe the church will go through the tribulation (postribulationists), and those who believe the church will be raptured prior to the tribulation (pretribulationists) and even a few who believe the church will be raptured in the middle of the tribulation (midtribulationists). Despite these differences in regard to the rapture of the church, premillennialists generally believe in the future restoration of the state of Israel and the eventual conversion of the Jews to Christianity.

The Jewish people who will be saved during the tribulation period are called the "144,000 servants of God" from "all the tribes of the children of Israel" (Revelation 7:4). The number seems to be literal, but it could also be symbolic of totality (i.e., national conversion of the Jews). There is no indication in the text that they are to be viewed as the New Testament church or Gentile Christians. They are said to be living on earth and need to be sealed in order to be protected from the judgments that are coming on the earth. When we consider the symbolism of the "woman" (Israel) and the "remnant of her seed" (converted Jews) in Revelation 12:1-17, it is clear that the 144,000 are literal Israelites. In fact, Revelation 7:5-8 specifically lists the fact that 12,000 come from each of the twelve tribes of Israel, which are listed in order.

The actual listing of the tribes would be irrelevant if they were not intended to represent the specific people of Israel. The specification of the tribes is consistent only with a literal interpretation of those tribes. John Walvoord writes: "The fact that the twelve tribes of Israel are singled out for special reference in the tribulation time is another evidence that the term 'Israel' as used in the Bible is invariably a reference to the descendants of Jacob who was first given the name Israel."[9]

Having listed 144,000 Jews (12,000 from each of the 12 tribes), John says, "After this ... " (Greek, *meta tauta*). This is John's typical literary expression to move the reader on to the next event, or, in this case, the next group. The innumerable multitude are not Jews from the twelve tribes of Israel. They are a host of people from every nation (Gentiles and Jews) and are so great in number they cannot humanly be counted.

John specifically identifies this group as coming from every nation (Greek, *ethnos*, "ethnic" group), kindreds (Greek, *phylon*, "family" groups), people (Greek, *laon*, "people" groups), and tongue (Greek, *glosson*, "language" group). The partitive e*k* ("from") means only some from every one of these groups will be represented. That this is a body of redeemed people is obvious from the fact that they stand before the Lamb in white robes (righteousness), waving palm branches (victory).

The text itself tells us who they are: "These are they which came out of great tribulation" (Revelation 7:14 KJV). They are also pictured as already standing before the throne of God, serving

Him day and night in the heavenly temple (Revelation 7:15). This innumerable multitude is a group of saved people, mostly Gentiles, who are already in heaven praising God. There is no specific reference to their having been martyred to get there. The fact that one of the elders (representing the church) asked who they are (Revelation 7:13) implies they are not Church Age saints.

This multitude represents the tribulation period believers who have come to faith in Christ. Non-pretribulationalists say this is the church of Jesus Christ, persecuted, martyred, and betrayed down through the centuries of church history. To hold this position, they must view the great tribulation as the entire Church Age.

Pretribulationalists believe, as the text says, that these are people who have been saved on earth during the tribulation period (first six seals) and "came out of" (Greek, *ek*, "from") the great tribulation (seventh seal and following). In other words, they have apparently died during the first half of the tribulation period and have been taken from the earth prior to the great tribulation.[10]

Divine Wrath and Great Tribulation

The great tribulation (Greek, *tes thlipseōs tēs megalēs*) refers to that eschatological period of God's wrath. It is not merely the persecution or "troubles" of John's own time but a time of future global retribution, called in Revelation 3:10 the "hour of trial" and, in 6:16, "the wrath of the Lamb."

Understanding the nature of these judgments is crucial to one's interpretation of the apocalypse. If the judgments of the tribulation period are something less than divine wrath, one might better argue for the church's remaining on earth during the tribulation. But there are two glaring contradictions to that viewpoint: 1) This is divine wrath; and 2) The multitude is already in heaven, but the tribulation judgments are not yet finished.

The church is pictured in Revelation 19:7-10 as the bride of Christ. She is in heaven at the marriage supper of the Lamb. She is also preparing to return to earth with Him in His ultimate triumph (19:11-16). She is the object of His love, not His wrath. She may be disciplined, corrected, or rebuked in the days of her earthly sojourn (Revelation 3:19). But she is *never* the object of His wrath! He cannot pour out divine wrath on the church because the Father poured out divine wrath on Jesus Christ on the cross. He already took the punishment of divine wrath for us (see Isaiah 53:1-12; 2 Corinthians 5:17-21; Hebrews 9:24-28; 10:5-25). He is our perfect substitute. He paid the price in full. "There is therefore now no condemnation to them which are in Christ Jesus" (Romans 8:1 KJV).

There is no logical way to explain how these judgments are the wrath of the Lamb while allowing them to fall on His bride. He wouldn't be much of a husband if He beat her up and then took her to the wedding reception! I believe that the church, the bride of Christ, has already been raptured home to glory.

There will be people converted during the tribulation period. While the witness of the church and its restraining force in society is missing, the omnipresent Holy Spirit will still convict men of sin, righteousness, and judgment (John 16:7-11). It is true that many will believe a lie (literally, "the lie") and be deceived by "strong delusion" (2 Thessalonians 2:10-12). Nevertheless, we see both Jewish and Gentile converts believing in Jesus as their Savior in Revelation 7. No wonder they "cried out" (literally, "keep on crying"), "Salvation to our God" (Revelation 7:10).

Revelation 7 ends with all of heaven on its face before God. His sovereignty is extolled in His redemption of Israel and the Gentiles alike, just as it was extolled in His divine act of creation (Revelation 4:11). What a powerful and beautiful picture! God is the one who saves people:

1. Before the Law (Abraham and the patriarchs)

2. Under the Law (Old Testament believers)

3. During the Church Age (New Testament church)

4. During the tribulation period (Tribulation saints)

5. During the millennial kingdom (Kingdom saints)

Salvation is a free gift of God's grace. It is secured for all believers from every age by the sacrificial and substitutionary death of Christ on the cross. It was there that He bore our sins and endured the wrath of God against us. In those awful moments, suspended between heaven and earth, the cup of divine judgment fell upon Him. He who knew no sin was made sin for us, that we might receive the righteousness of God as a free gift (2 Corinthians 5:17-21). In His death on the cross, He triumphed over sin, death, and hell. No wonder He shouted, "It is finished!"

Salvation is possible after the rapture. Many Jews and Gentiles will be saved during that terrible time on earth. But most of them will lose their lives for the cause of Christ. The vast majority of people who are left behind after the rapture will be deceived by the antichrist and the false prophet, and that delusion will condemn them forever (2 Thessalonians 2:10-12). Don't take any chances with your eternal destiny. Make sure you are ready to go when Jesus comes to call us home to heaven.

What Will Happen
When Christ Returns?

The second coming of Christ is the most anticipated event in human history. It is the ultimate fulfillment of our Lord's promise to return. It is also the culmination of all biblical prophecy. The return of Christ is the final apologetic! Once He returns, there will be no further need to debate His claims or the validity of the Christian message. The King will come in person to set the record straight.

Revelation 19 is probably the most dramatic chapter in all the Bible. It is the capstone to the death and resurrection of Christ. In this chapter the living Savior returns to earth to crush all satanic opposition to the truth. He establishes His kingdom on earth in fulfillment of the Old Testament prophecies and of His own promise to return.

Just before the crucifixion, the disciples asked Jesus, "What shall be the sign of thy coming?" (Matthew 24:3 KJV). Our Lord replied, "Immediately after the tribulation of those days ... the powers of the heavens shall be shaken: and then shall appear the sign of the Son of man in heaven: and then shall all the tribes of the earth mourn, and they shall see the Son of man coming in the clouds of heaven with power and great glory" (Matthew 24:29-30).

As Jesus looked down the corridor of time to the end of the present age, He warned of a time of great tribulation that would come upon the whole world (Matthew 24:5-28). Our Lord went on to explain that the devastation of the great tribulation will be so extensive that unless those days were cut short, "no one would survive" (Matthew 24:22). Jesus further described this coming day of trouble as a time when the sun and moon will be darkened and the heavens will be shaken (Matthew 24:29). His description runs parallel to that found in Revelation 16:1-16, where the final hour of the tribulation is depicted by atmospheric darkness, air pollution, and ecological disaster.

The return of Christ is a twofold event. It marks both the final defeat of the antichrist and the final triumph of Christ. Rene Pache writes: "The main event announced by the prophets is not the judgment of the world, nor the restoration of Israel, nor even the triumph of the church: it is the glorious advent of the Son of God."[1] Without Him, there is no hope of a better future. He is the central figure of the world to come. It is His kingdom, and we are His bride. Oh, what a day that will be!

The Promise of His Return

Jesus promised His disciples in the upper room that He was going to heaven to prepare a place for them. Then He said, "If I go and prepare a place for you, I will come again, and receive you unto myself; that where I am, there ye may be also" (John 14:3 KJV). Even though the early disciples eventually died, the Bible promised, "Behold I shew you a mystery; we shall not all sleep [die], but we shall all be changed [resurrected or raptured], in a moment, in the twinkling of an eye, at the last trump: for the trumpet shall sound, and the dead shall be raised incorruptible, and we shall be changed" (1 Corinthians 15:51-52 KJV).

The apostle Paul reiterates this same hope in 1 Thessalonians 4:13-17, when he comments about those believers who have already died and gone to heaven. He says, "For if we believe that Jesus died and rose again, even so them also which sleep [die] in Jesus will God bring with him [from heaven].... For the Lord himself shall descend from heaven with a shout, with the voice of the archangel, and with the trump of God: and the dead in Christ shall rise first: then we which are alive and remain shall be caught up together with them in the clouds, to meet the Lord in the air."

The promise to return for the church (believers of the Church Age) is the promise of the rapture. When Revelation 19 opens, the church is already in heaven with Christ at the marriage supper. The rapture has already occurred. Jesus is depicted as the groom and the church as the bride. The marriage supper celebrates their union after the rapture and before their return to earth.

One of the greatest interpretive problems for nonrapturists is to explain *how* the church got to heaven *prior* to the second coming! Surely they were not all martyred, or else Paul's comment about "we which are alive and remain" (1 Thessalonians 4:15) would be meaningless! The rapture must be presumed to have occurred *before* the events in Revelation 19—amillennialists and postmillennialists notwithstanding!

The position of the church (bride of the Lamb) in Revelation 19:7-10 *in heaven* is crucial to the interpretation of the entire apocalypse. New Testament scholar Robert Gromacki points out: "The church is not mentioned during the seal, trumpet, and bowl judgments because the church is not here during the outpouring of these judgments."[2] He points out that the term *church* (Greek, *ekklesia*) appears frequently in chapters 1–3 of the Revelation. In fact, it is used nineteen times in those chapters. But the word *church* does not appear again until 22:16. In the meantime, the church appears in 19:7-10 as the bride of the Lamb.

The concept of the church as the bride or wife of Christ is clearly stated in Ephesians 5:22-23, where husbands are admonished to love their wives as Christ loved the church and gave Himself for her that He might present her in heaven as a glorious bride. There can be no doubt, therefore, that John intends us to see the Lamb's "wife" as the church—the bride of Christ.

The Nature of Christ's Return

Jesus not only promised to return for His church; He also promised to return to judge the world and to establish His kingdom on earth. His brother James refers to believers as "heirs of the kingdom which he hath promised to them that love him" (James 2:5 KJV). Jesus Himself told His disciples that He would not drink the fruit of the vine after the last supper until He drank it with them in His Father's kingdom (Matthew 26:29). After the resurrection, they asked Him, "Wilt thou at this time restore again the kingdom to Israel?" (Acts 1:6). He replied that the time was in the Father's hand. All these references imply a future kingdom when Christ returns.

The details of ***Christ's return*** include the following aspects:

1. *He will return personally.* The Bible promises that "the Lord himself shall descend from Heaven" (1 Thessalonians 4:16). Jesus promised He Himself will return in person (Matthew 24:30).

2. *He will appear as the Son of man.* Since Pentecost, Christ has ministered through the Holy Spirit (John 14:16-23; 16:7-20). But when He returns, He will appear as the Son of man in His glorified human form (Matthew 24:30; 26:64; Daniel 7:13-14).

3. *He will return literally and visibly.* In Acts 1:11, the angels promised, "This same Jesus, which is taken up from you into heaven, shall so come in like manner." Revelation 1:7 tells us, "Every eye shall see him, and they also which pierced him: and all kindreds of the earth" (KJV).

4. *He will come suddenly and dramatically.* Paul warned, "The day of the Lord will come like a thief in the night" (1 Thessalonians 5:2). Jesus said, "For as the lightning cometh out of the east, and shineth even unto the west; so shall also the coming of the Son of man be" (Matthew 24:27).

5. *He will come on the clouds of heaven.* Jesus said, "They shall see the Son of man coming in the clouds of heaven" (Matthew 24:30). Daniel 7:13 predicts the same thing. So does Luke 21:27. Revelation 1:7 says, "Behold, he cometh with clouds."

6. *He will come in a display of glory.* Matthew 16:27 promises, "The Son of man shall come in the glory of his Father." Matthew 24:30 adds, "They shall see the Son of man coming ... with power and great glory."

7. *He will come with all His angels.* Jesus promised, "And he shall send his angels with a great sound of a trumpet" (Matthew 24:31). Jesus said in one of His parables, "The reapers are the angels.... So shall it be in the end of this world" (Matthew 13:39-40 KJV).

8. *He will come with His bride—the church.* That, of course, is the whole point of Revelation 19. Colossians 3:4 adds, "When Christ ... shall appear, then shall ye also appear with him in glory." Zechariah 14:5 adds, "And the Lord my God shall come, and all the saints with thee."

9. *He will return to the Mount of Olives.* "And his feet shall stand in that day upon the mount of Olives" (Zechariah 14:4). Where the glory of God ascended

into heaven, it will return (Ezekiel 11:23). Where Jesus ascended into heaven, He will return (Acts 1:3-12).

10. *He will return in triumph and victory.* Zechariah 14:9 promises, "And the Lord shall be king over all the earth" (KJV). Revelation 19:16 depicts him as "King of kings and Lord of lords." He will triumph over the antichrist, the false prophet, and Satan himself (Revelation 19:19-21).

Hallelujah, What a Savior!

Revelation 19 opens with a heavenly chorus of "many people" singing the praises of God (verse 1). G.R. Beasley-Murray calls it a *"Te Deum* on the righteous judgments of God."[3] The heavenly choir rejoices with praise because justice has finally been served. "True and righteous are his judgments," they sing, because "he hath judged the great whore" (Revelation 19:2). The praise chorus then breaks into a *fourfold hallelujah* ("alleluia," KJV) in verses 1-6:

1. "Hallelujah! Salvation and glory and power belong to our God" (verse 1).

2. Hallelujah! "He has condemned the great prostitute" (verses 2-3).

3. They "worshipped God…on the throne, saying, Amen; Hallelujah" (verse 4).

4. Hallelujah! "for our Lord God Almighty reigns." Hallelujah! (verse 6).

This is the only place in the New Testament where *hallelujah* occurs. It is a Hebrew word ("Praise Yah," or *Jehovah*). It was transliterated from the Hebrew into Greek and passed on into English. The same thing occurred with *amen, hosanna,* and *maranatha.* The use of the four "hallelujahs" emphasizes the magnitude of this praise and worship.

Beasley-Murray observes that these "hallelujahs" are reminiscent of the *Hallel Psalms* (113–118) which were sung at the Jewish Passover meal.[4] The first two (113–114) were sung before the meal and the rest after the meal. Just as Israel sang God's praises for His deliverance in the Passover, so the church in heaven sings God's praise for His deliverance from the antichrist. But the triumph that is heralded focuses on the marriage of the Lamb that takes center stage in this cantata of praise.

Marriage Supper of the Lamb

The marriage of the Lamb is announced suddenly and dramatically. It is as though we have finally arrived at what we have been waiting for all along. The wedding is finally here. It is obvious that John the revelator views this as a future (not past) event. The final culmination of their spiritual union has finally arrived.

Beasley-Murray expresses it like this: "The perfection in glory of the bride belongs to the eschatological future. In this figure, therefore, the *now* and the *not yet* of the New Testament doctrine of salvation in the Kingdom of God is perfectly exemplified. The church is the Bride of Christ now, but her marriage lies in the future."[5]

This is exactly why we cannot say that the consummation of the marriage has already taken place. The apostle Paul writes, "For I have espoused you to one husband, that I may present you as a chaste virgin to Christ" (2 Corinthians 11:2 KJV). He also adds that Christ "loved the church, and gave himself for it … that he might present it to himself a glorious church, not having spot, or wrinkle, or any such thing; but that it should be holy and without blemish" (Ephesians 5:25-27 KJV).

Bruce Metzger comments: "The concept of the relationship between God and his people as a marriage goes far back into the

Old Testament. Again and again the prophets spoke of Israel as the chosen bride of God (Isaiah 54:1-8; Ezekiel 16:7,8; Hosea 2:19). In the New Testament the church is represented as the bride of Christ.... In the words of a familiar hymn: 'With his own blood he bought her, and for her life he died.'"[6]

The New Testament pictures the church as engaged to Christ by faith at this present time. We are still awaiting the "judgment seat of Christ" (2 Corinthians 5:10), presumably after the rapture and before the marriage supper. The marriage ceremony itself will follow in heaven during the tribulation period on earth. Dwight Pentecost writes, "At the translation of the church, Christ is appearing as a a bridegroom to take his bride unto Himself, so that the relationship that was pledged might be consummated and the two might become one."[7]

Christ is still pictured symbolically as the Lamb (19:7), but the picture of the marriage is clearly expressed. The aorist tense of "is come" (Greek, *elthen*) indicates a completed act, showing that the wedding is now consummated. Instead of the normal seven-day Jewish wedding ceremony, this one presumably lasts seven years (during the tribulation period). The marriage is completed in heaven (Revelation 19:7), but the marriage supper probably takes place later on earth where Israel is awaiting the return of Christ and the church.

This is the only way to distinguish the Bridegroom (Christ), the bride (church), and the ten virgins (Israel) in the passage in Matthew 25:1-13. There is no way that He is coming to marry all ten (or five) of these women. They are the attendants (Old Testament saints and tribulation saints) at the wedding. Only the church is the bride. That is how Jesus could say of John the Baptist that there was not a "greater prophet" (Old Testament saint), but he that is "least in the kingdom of God" (New Testament church) is "greater than he" (Luke 7:28).

The Triumphal Return

The singular vignette of Christ's return in Revelation 19:11-16 is the most dramatic passage in all the Bible! In these six verses we are swept up into the triumphal entourage of redeemed saints as they ride in the heavenly procession with the King of kings and Lord of lords. In this one passage alone, all the hopes and dreams of every believer are finally and fully realized. This is not the Palm Sunday procession with the humble Messiah on the donkey colt. This is the ultimate in eschatological drama. The rejected Savior returns in triumph as the rightful King of all the world—and *we* are with Him.

Metzger notes: "From here on the tempo of the action increases. The ultimate outcome cannot be in doubt, but there are some surprises ahead, with the suspense of the drama sustained to the conclusion. From verse 11 to the first verse of chapter 21, we have in rapid succession seven visions preparatory to the end. Each of these begins with the words, 'I saw.'"[8]

The description of the triumphant Savior is that of a king leading an army to victory. The passage itself is the final phase of the seventh bowl of judgment begun in Revelation 16:17-21, moving through the details of 17:1–18:24 and on to chapter 19.

As the scene unfolds, heaven opens to reveal the Christ and to release the army of the redeemed. The description of their being clad in white (verse 14) emphasizes the garments of the bride already mentioned earlier (verse 8). In this vignette, the bride appears as the army of the Messiah. But unlike contemporary apocalyptic dramas of that time (e.g., War Scroll of the Qumran sect), the victory is won without any military help from the faithful. This army has no weapons, no swords, no shields, no armor. They are merely clad in the "righteousness of the saints." They have not come to fight, but to watch. They have not come to assist, but to celebrate. The Messiah-King will do the fighting. He alone will win the battle by the power of His spoken word.

The *twelve-fold description* of the *coming King* combines elements of symbolism from various biblical passages and from the previous pictures of the risen Christ in the revelation itself. Notice the details of His appearance:

1. He rides the white horse (Revelation 6:2).

2. He is called faithful and true (Revelation 3:14).

3. He judges and makes war in righteousness (2 Thessalonians 1:7-8).

4. His eyes are as a flame of fire (Revelation 1:14).

5. He wears many crowns (Revelation 12:3; 13:1).

6. His name is unknown—a wonderful secret (Judges 13:18; Isaiah 9:6).

7. He is clothed in a robe dipped in blood (Isaiah 63:1-6).

8. His name is called the Word of God (John 1:1).

9. A sharp sword is in His mouth (Hebrews 4:12).

10. He rules with a rod of iron (Psalm 2:9; Isaiah 11:4).

11. He treads the winepress of the wrath of God (Isaiah 63:1-6; Revelation 14:14-20).

12. His written name is King of kings and Lord of lords (Daniel 2:47; Revelation 17:14).

There can be no doubt that the rider on the white horse (19:11-16) is Jesus Christ. He comes as the apostle Paul predicted: "in flaming fire taking vengeance on them that know not God…who shall be punished with everlasting destruction… when he shall come to be glorified in his saints, and to be admired in all them that believe" (2 Thessalonians 1:8-10 KJV).

This is the true Christ (Messiah) not the usurper (antichrist). He rides the white horse of conquest, and the outcome of His victory is sure. His greatness is in the spiritual qualities of His person: faithful, true, righteous. His eyes of fire penetrate our sinfulness and expose our spiritual inadequacy. His "many crowns" were probably received from those of the redeemed who cast them at his feet in worship (Revelation 4:10). The fact that these crowns (*diadems*) are "many" totally upstages the seven crowns of the dragon (Revelation 12:3) and the ten crowns of the beast (Revelation 13:1). His unknown name is a "secret" or "wonder" (see Judges 13:18 and Isaiah 9:6). He is Jehovah God Himself— the *Yahweh* (YHVH) of the Old Testament. He is the I AM whose name is "above every name" (Philippians 2:9-11).

John wants us to know for certain who this is, so he calls Him by his favorite name: the Word (Greek, *logos*) of God (see John 1:1). He is the self-disclosure of the Almighty. He is the personal revelation of God to man. He is the personal Word who is also the author of the written word. The One revealed is the ultimate revelator of the revelation: Jesus the Christ.

The Savior returns from heaven with His bride at His side. The church militant is now the church triumphant. Her days of conflict, rejection, and persecution are over. She returns victorious with her Warrior-King-Husband. The German Pietist A.W. Boehm put it best when he wrote:

> There will be a time when the church of Christ will come up from the wilderness of her crosses and afflictions, leaning upon her Beloved, and in his power bidding defiance to all her enemies. Then shall the church...appear Terrible as an Army with banners; but terrible to those only that despised her while she was in her minority, and would not have her Beloved to reign over them.[9]

Every true believer who reads the prediction of Christ's triumph in Revelation 19:11-16 is overwhelmed by its significance. We are also overcome by its personal implications, for each of us will be in that heavenly army that returns with Him from Glory. In fact, you might want to take a pen and circle the word *armies* in 19:14 and write your name in the margin of your Bible next to it, for *you* will be there when He returns!

The destiny of the true believer is now fully clarified. Our future hope includes: 1) Rapture; 2) Return; and 3) Reign. No matter what one's eschatological viewpoint, the church must be raptured (Greek, *harpazō,* "caught up") to heaven prior to the marriage supper and prior to her return from heaven with Christ. In the rapture, we go up to heaven. In the return, we come back to earth. In the millennium, we reign with Christ on the earth for a thousand years (Revelation 20:4).

The Last Battle

Revelation 19 ends with the final triumph of Christ over the antichrist, presumably at or after the battle of Armageddon. The passage itself merely refers to the carnage as the "supper of the great God" (Revelation 19:17 KJV). While Armageddon is only mentioned by name in Revelation 16:16, that one reference introduces the final conflict that is called the "battle of that great day of God Almighty" (Revelation 16:14 KJV). This includes the sounding of the seventh trumpet (Revelation 16:17), the great earthquake (16:18-20), and the fall of "Babylon" (17:1–19:6).

The closing verses of chapter 19 (verses 17-21) summarize the final concluding events of the battle of Armageddon. Notice the pattern of Revelation is always panorama followed by snapshots. First the big picture, then the details. The end of the chapter concludes all that has been happening since the first mention of Armageddon in 16:16.

The antichrist (beast), the kings of the earth, and their combined armies are "gathered" against Christ and the church to make war. The term *gathered* (Greek, *sunagoge*) in 19:19 is the same word used in 16:16 in relation to Armageddon. Therefore, it is clear that this is still the same conflict. As we noted earlier, Armageddon may actually be a war of which this is the final battle. The carnage is so extensive that it includes kings, captains, mighty men, cavalry, small men, and great men (19:18).

Christ returns with His church, but not to spare His church. He returns to spare the human race. He Himself predicted that "except those days should be shortened, there should no flesh be saved" (Matthew 24:22). Now, He returns in triumph and wins the battle by the power of His spoken word (sword "of his mouth," verse 21). He but speaks and the battle is over! Just as He spoke, "Peace, be still" and the storm ceased (Mark 4:39), so the greatest conflagration in human history comes to an end—just in time. Jesus the Messiah triumphs by the divine word. He who spoke the worlds into existence speaks and the enemy is slain. The battle is over, and Christ and His church are at last victorious.

The chapter ends with the beast (antichrist) and the false prophet defeated. Both are cast alive into the lake of fire. This punishment dramatizes the seriousness of their offense and the finality of Christ's victory over them. The rest of the rebel army is slain, but they are not consigned to the lake of fire until the great white throne judgment (Revelation 20:11-15). The fact that the beast and the false prophet are cast *alive* into the lake of fire, and that they are still there in Revelation 20:10, indicates that it is a place of eternal conscious punishment.

The two prophetic aorists (*taken* and *cast*) predict the capture and consignment of the two superhuman enemies of Christ. In the meantime, Revelation 20:1-2 tells us that Satan will be bound in the bottomless pit for 1,000 years before he, too, is cast into the lake of fire. In each case, it is Christ who sends them into the lake of fire, not Satan. Jesus alone will determine the final judgment of unbelievers, as well as of the unholy trinity.

As dramatic and climactic as this chapter is, it only sets the stage for the millennium and the eternal state that are to follow. The marriage of the Lamb began with the opening ceremonies in heaven. Now the King and His bride will rule for 1,000 years on earth. During this time, all of God's promised blessings to Israel will be literally fulfilled as the devastated earth again blossoms like a rose.

Will There Be a Literal Kingdom on Earth?

The idea of the kingdom of God on earth is central to all biblical teaching. The Old Testament prophets predicted it. Jesus announced it. And the New Testament apostles foretold it again. The psalmist said, "God is my King" (Psalm 74:12). Jeremiah said of the Lord, "He is a living God, and an everlasting king" (Jeremiah 10:10). John the revelator refers to Jesus Christ as "King of kings and Lord of lords" (Revelation 19:16).

The concept of the *kingdom* is closely associated with that of the King. Daniel wrote, "The most High ruleth in the kingdom of men" (Daniel 4:17 KJV). The psalmist adds, "His kingdom ruleth over all" (Psalm 103:19 KJV). George Ladd observes, "The primary meaning of the New Testament word for *Kingdom, basileia,* is 'reign' rather than 'realm' or 'people.' ... In the general linguistic usage ... *basileia* ... designates first of all the existence, the character, the position of the King."[1]

There can be no true kingdom without a king. God has always chosen human representatives to mediate His kingdom on earth. The rule of God through such mediators is called a "theocratic" kingdom. Alva McClain defines such a kingdom as "the rule of God through a divinely chosen representative who speaks and acts for God."[2]

The kingdom of God has always existed, and it will always exist. It is the sovereign rule of God from eternity past to eternity future. It has been mediated on earth through the dominion of man over the creation and through the divine institution of human government. In relation to the nation of Israel, the kingdom of God was to be administered by divinely appointed kings in the Davidic line (the line of the Messiah). But only with the coming of the Messiah will the hopes and dreams of a kingdom of God on earth be fully realized.

William S. LaSor states: "The messianic Kingdom on earth is a vindication of God's creative activity.... The triumph of God over the satanic dominion of this planet is necessary for the glory of God. If there were no Messianic Age, if God simply picked up the redeemed remnant and took them off to heaven, then we would have to conclude that God was unable to complete what He began."[3]

The kingdom of God on earth reaches its apex during the 1,000-year reign of Christ. The term *millennium* comes from the Latin words *mille* ("thousand") and *annus* ("year"). Thus, it refers to the thousand-year reign of Christ. John Walvoord notes, "The Greek word for millennium comes from *chilias*, meaning 'a thousand.' The Greek term is used six times in the original text of the twentieth chapter of Revelation to define the duration of Christ's Kingdom on earth."[4]

The Messianic Age

The Old Testament prophets foretold a *golden era* of peace and prosperity when the Messiah would rule on earth. Isaiah wrote:

> And it shall come to pass in the last days, that the mountain of the Lord's house shall be established ... and all nations shall flow unto it ... for out of Zion shall go forth the law, and the word of the Lord from Jerusalem. And he shall judge among the nations ... and they shall beat their swords into plowshares, and their spears into pruning hooks: nation shall not lift up sword against nation, neither shall they learn war any more (Isaiah 2:2-4 KJV).

God's promises to Israel include her earthly and spiritual blessings. This explains why the disciples asked Jesus, "Lord, are you at this time going to restore the kingdom to Israel?" (Acts 1:6). This question was raised after the resurrection and before the ascension. It reveals that the Jewish disciples were still looking for the promised Messianic kingdom. Little did they realize that Jesus was about to return to heaven and postpone that phase of the kingdom until the distant future.

"It is not for you to know the times or dates the Father has set by his own authority," Jesus replied (Acts 1:7). He did not say there would be no future kingdom. He merely indicated that it would come later. In the meantime, He commissioned the disciples to go into all the world and preach the gospel.

During the Church Age, the kingdom of God is "within" us (Luke 17:21). Jesus said it does not come with "observation" (Luke 17:20). We become citizens of that kingdom by faith in Jesus Christ as our King. Thus, our citizenship is in heaven (see Philippians 3:20). In the meantime, we are Christ's ambassadors on earth, commissioned to proclaim the gospel to all nations.

As premillennialists, we look forward to the rapture of the church. We have no pretensions of being able to bring in the kingdom on earth by our own efforts. This has always been the position of postmillennialists in general, and it is destined to utter failure. If the church must bring in the kingdom, we will be a long time awaiting its arrival. In fact, by all current measures, we are desperately falling behind.

Beyond the rapture, we do look forward to the fulfillment of the Messianic Age. We believe the kingdom of God will come on earth when the King comes back to rule. In the meantime, we continue to declare Him as King and His gospel as the means of salvation. Jesus Himself told us to do this when He said, "And this gospel of the kingdom will be preached in the whole world for a testimony to all nations, and then the end will come" (Matthew 24:14).

The Binding of Satan

Revelation 20 opens with an angel descending from heaven with the key to the abyss (KJV "bottomless pit"). He is also described as carrying a "great chain" by which he bound Satan for "a thousand years" (Revelation 20:1). Then the angel cast him into the abyss and sealed it shut for the duration of that time.

Robert Mounce observes: "The purpose of the confinement is not punishment. It is to prevent him from deceiving the nations. The elaborate measures taken to insure his custody are most easily understood as implying the complete cessation of his influence on earth, rather than a curbing of his activities."[5] This point is crucial to one's interpretation of the binding of Satan for 1,000 years. Amillennial commentators try to say this is descriptive of the present age. They hold that Satan is currently "bound" and his influence on earth is limited by the power of the gospel. In order to think this, they must view the 1,000 years as figurative of the entire Church Age.

John Walvoord points out the problem with this viewpoint when he writes, "Opposed to the amillennial interpretation, however, is the uniform revelation of the New Testament which shows Satan is a very active person. If anything, he is more active than in preceding ages and is continuing an unrelenting opposition to all that God purposes to do in the present age."[6]

Walvoord cites numerous examples of *Satan's current activity:*

1. He is the god of this world (2 Corinthians 4:4).

2. He blinds the minds of the lost (2 Corinthians 4:3-4).

3. He is the prince of the power of the air (Ephesians 2:2).

4. He appears as an angel of light (2 Corinthians 11:14).

5. He walks about like a roaring lion (1 Peter 5:8).

These passages make it clear that Satan is anything but bound during the present age. All attempts to picture him otherwise seem rather ludicrous. Therefore, the binding of Satan must be a future event that has not yet occurred. Its relationship to the 1,000 years indicates a literal, rather than symbolic, period of time. We call this period, therefore, the millennial kingdom. Thomas Ice and Timothy Demy write, "Even though the Bible speaks descriptively throughout about the millennial Kingdom, it was not until the final book—Revelation—that the length of His Kingdom is revealed."[7]

While the 1,000 years may be symbolic of a long time of peace and prosperity, there is nothing in the text itself to indicate that this period should not be taken literally. Otherwise, all other time indicators in Revelation would be meaningless. Harold Hoehner writes: "The denial of a literal 1,000 years is not because of the exegesis of the text but a predisposition brought to the text."[8]

Attempts to "spiritualize" the thousand years as symbolic often go hand in hand with attempts to "spiritualize" the biblical promises of a glorious future to the nation of Israel. No less a theologian than T.F. Torrance of the University of Edinburgh, Scotland, has said: "The historical particularity of Israel covenanted with God persists through the Christian era. God has not cast off His ancient people (Romans 11); for the covenant with Israel as God's people remains in force, and cannot be 'spiritualized' and turned into some form alien to the stubborn historicity of its nature without calling into question the whole historical foundation of God's revelation."[9]

Ruling with Christ on Earth

Beasley-Murray writes: "The essential element of the idea of the millennium is the appearing of the Kingdom of the Messiah in history, prior to the revelation of the Kingdom of God in the eternal and transcendent realm of the new creation."[10] In this regard, Revelation 19 provides a transition from the fall of "Babylon" (city of man) to the arrival of the new Jerusalem (city of God).

There is no detailed description of the millennial reign here. For that we must rely on the Old Testament prophets. John focuses only on the fact that we will rule with Christ on earth— a promise he introduced earlier in Revelation 5:10. There the text says, "And hast made us ... kings and priests: and we shall reign on the earth" (KJV). Thus, the idea of a literal earthly kingdom has already been introduced as a future prospect. Now it is portrayed as a present reality.

John foresees the tribulation martyrs ruling with Christ in the millennial kingdom. He also sees "thrones" and those seated on them to whom judgment was given. The scene is similar to the one described by Daniel (7:9-10,22). While it is possible that these are the thrones of the twenty-four elders, they are not specified as such (see Revelation 4:4; 5:8-10; 7:13; 11:15). Since Jesus promised the twelve apostles they would sit on thrones judging the twelve tribes of Israel (see Matthew 19:28; Luke 22:30), it seems likely that would be in view here during the earthly kingdom.

The total picture is much greater. The bride (church) has returned from heaven with Christ in chapter 19. Now the "tribulation saints" (believers) are resurrected to rule with them. This is called the "first resurrection" (Revelation 20:5) to distinguish it from the second resurrection, in which the dead are brought to judgment after the 1,000 years (Revelation 20:11-15).

The martyrs are described as those who were beheaded for the witness of Jesus and for the word of God, and had not worshiped the beast or his image nor received his mark (Revelation 20:4). The unsaved dead remain dead for the entire 1,000 years. But the martyrs are resurrected to rule with Christ during the millennial kingdom. This privilege is the reward for their faithfulness to Christ in the face of unprecedented persecution. During this time, the damage of the tribulation period will be reversed and the earth will prosper under the personal reign of Christ on the throne of David (see Zechariah 12:10; Isaiah 9:6-7). Without such a rule, the return of Christ would be only a "walk among the ruins" after the battle of Armageddon.[11]

In one of the great surprises of the apocalyptic drama, Satan is loosed from the abyss after the millennium. John the revelator provides no specific details as to who, how, or why this occurs. He merely records, "When the thousand years are over, Satan will be released from his prison and will go out to deceive the nations" (Revelation 20:7-8).

Several things are apparent in this account:

1. Some nations survive the tribulation period and live into the millennium.

2. Children continue to be born to the people of earth during the millennium.

3. Christ rules during the millennium with a rod of iron.

4. Mankind rebels against Christ despite the blessing of the millennium.

The final revolt is the ultimate proof of human depravity. Unredeemed minds will tolerate Christ's rule, but they will not bow their hearts to Him. As soon as Satan is loosed, they rebel against the rule of God. Even though Edenic conditions have been restored to earth, mankind once again falls prey to the deceiver.

Beasley-Murray writes: "The full potential of human existence cannot be attained within the limitations of this world, even in the most idyllic conditions, in view of the unceasing possibilities for evil which exist within it."[12]

While some are surprised—even shocked—by this revolt, we must remember two things have not changed: *unrepentant* Satan and *unregenerate* mankind. The devil is still the deceiver, the "father of lies." He will not cease from his destructive ways. He has not repented after 1,000 years in the abyss. Therefore, God's only possible act of mercy to the rest of the world is to cast him into the lake of fire (Revelation 19:10). Notice, it is God, not Satan, who ultimately condemns people to eternal damnation (see Revelation 19:20; 20:9-10, 12-15).

The *final battle* involves "Gog and Magog" (Revelation 20:8). It comes after the millennium and involves many nations attacking the "camp of the saints" and the "beloved city"—presumably Jerusalem. This final act of rebellion is squelched by fire that comes down from God out of heaven. The imagery is typical of Jewish apocalyptic writings (see 2 Esdras 13:1-12). The reference to Gog and Magog is similar to Ezekiel 28–29, a passage often interpreted to occur before the millennium. Whether John's usage is identical to Ezekiel or only similar to it is a matter of debate.[13]

The idea expressed in Revelation is that the unrepentant and unredeemed nations have been deceived into thinking they can attack Christ and the saints successfully. After 1,000 years, the memory of His victory at Armageddon has faded sufficiently enough for them to even dare such an enterprise. But the greatest tragedy of all is that they will reject the Savior who has ruled in person for a thousand years. However, this should not surprise us in light of those who personally rejected Him at His first coming. They, too, said, "His blood be on us" (Matthew 27:25 KJV). The hearts of men are spiritually cold and dead apart from the regenerating power of God's Spirit. Those in the millennium will have every chance to believe, but some will remain lost despite their opportunities to be saved.

Satan is finally cast into the lake of fire, from which there is no escape or release (Revelation 20:10). The beast and the false prophet have already been there 1,000 years, being tormented day and night. Their condition emphasizes the seriousness of the eternal punishment of the damned. They are condemned forever with no hope of escape or release. That is why consignment there is called the "second death."

Great White Throne Judgment

Next, John sees a "great white throne." This is the judgment throne, not the royal throne. Heaven (atmosphere) and earth (planet) "fled away," and there was "found no place for them" (Revelation 20:11 KJV). Many assume it is at this point that the earth and its atmosphere are burned up and destroyed by fire (2 Peter 3:7-13). This will pave the way for the "new heavens" and "new earth." The earth and its atmosphere are dissolved, and the great white throne judgment takes place in space in eternity.

Robert Thomas reminds us, "A closer examination of most passages that allegedly teach one final judgment shows that *future judgment* will come in several phases":[14]

1. Judgment of the martyrs (Revelation 20:4-5)

2. Judgment of the nations (Matthew 25:31-46)

3. Judgment seat of Christ (2 Corinthians 5:10)

4. Great white throne judgment (Revelation 20:11-15)

This final judgment takes place after the millennium. It involves all the unsaved dead of all time ("small and great"). This is a judgment not of believers but of unbelievers. This judgment results in the condemnation of all who appear there.

God the Father is the Judge on this occasion. "Him that sat" (Revelation 20:11) on the throne is called "God" (20:12). Christ has judged the believers; now the Father judges the unbelievers. Written records of the deeds of all men are kept in books (Greek, *biblia*, "scrolls"). These accounts testify against all men that they have sinned. The Bible is clear in its emphasis on human accountability: "For all have sinned, and come short of the glory of God" (Romans 3:23 KJV). The idea of a written record of men's deeds is found elsewhere in Daniel 7:10, Isaiah 65:6, and Malachi 3:16.

These books of human deeds are only for the purpose of condemnation. They are not a basis for salvation by works. Indeed, no one can be saved by works (see Ephesians 2:8-10). These registers of deeds testify against us and our sins. The only hope for salvation is in another register—a list of names. It is the book of life (Greek, *biblion tes zoes*) which settles the eternal destiny of all men. Your name must be written there if you are to have any hope of heaven (see Revelation 3:5; 13:8; 17:8; 21:17).

The judgment of one's works also determines the degree of one's punishment. All who are condemned here are consigned to the lake of fire. No one escapes! Both death (*thanatos*) and hell (*hades*) are pictured as though they were the city jail, whereas the lake of fire is the penitentiary. Unsaved people go to hell when they die (Luke 16:19-24). But hell is not the end. It is only the holding place while they await final trial at the great white throne judgment. Afterward, the lost are consigned to the lake of fire. In fact, when the judgment is finally over, death and hell themselves are cast into the lake of fire. This is called the "second death" (Revelation 20:14).

There is no "hiding place" from God's final judgment. All the dead of all time are resurrected to stand trial before God almighty. Even hell is turned upside down and emptied out for this great and terrible judgment. There will be no excuses, no blaming of others, no pointing the finger. Each man and woman will stand alone at the great white throne. Each will give an account of himself or herself. And each will be condemned by his or her own record—a lifetime of sins for which there is no excuse.

Banishment from the presence of God will be the final result of this judgment. Consignment to the lake of fire will be forever. God has gone out of His way to give mankind every possible chance to repent, but this last act of rebellion after 1,000 years of blessing will mark the end of His patience. And all who have rejected Christ as Lord will be condemned to the lake of fire.

All the greatest efforts of mankind are burned up in the end. Armageddon nearly destroys the planet. Now this battle of Gog and Magog results in earth's final devastation. All the best efforts of the finest minds that have ever lived end in hopeless chaos without God. All is under His judgment. The Bible warns us, "It is a dreadful thing to fall into the hands of the living God" (Hebrews 10:31).

The final chapters of Revelation take us to the ultimate prophetic vision: eternity. Beyond the great tribulation and the millennial kingdom lies the final reality: the eternal state. There is a powerful reminder in these chapters that this present world is not the end. There is indeed a new world coming where God is in complete control. Even the blessings of the earthly millennium cannot compare with the glorious eternity that awaits the children of God.

11

The Final Reality:
The New Earth

The future is limitless. Beyond the great tribulation and the millennial kingdom lies the final reality: the eternal state. This is a powerful reminder that this present world is not the end. There is indeed a new world coming where God is in complete control. Even the blessings of the earthly millennium cannot compare with the glorious eternity that awaits the children of God.

John the revelator was not the first to see all the way down the canyon of eternity. Isaiah the prophet also foresaw new heavens and a new earth (Isaiah 65:17-25; 66:22-24). He even went so far as to say, "The former shall not be remembered, nor come into mind" (Isaiah 65:17 KJV). The apostle Peter, too, spoke of "new heavens and a new earth" (2 Peter 3:7-13 KJV). Peter said the present world is "reserved unto fire against the day of judgment" (3:7). He predicts a time when "the heavens shall pass away with a great noise, and the elements shall melt with fervent heat.... Nevertheless we, according to his promise, look for new heavens and a new earth, wherein dwelleth righteousness" (2 Peter 3:10,13 KJV).

Revelation 21 introduces us into a whole new series of events. We have entered the final phase of the apocalypse—eternity. All judgments are now concluded. God shall wipe away all tears from our eyes, and there shall be no more sorrow, nor death. Even during the blessings of the millennium, human sufferings were not totally eliminated. But in God's new world order, they are no more.

Wilbur Smith writes: "In Revelation 21:1–22:5 we have the most extensive revelation of the eternal home of the redeemed to be found anywhere in the Scriptures, and most suitably it forms the conclusion of all the revelation of the ages recorded in our Bible. The remaining verses (Revelation 22:6-21) are simply an appendix including an exhortation, warning and promise."[1]

John begins his final vision with the familiar words "and I saw" (Revelation 21:1), reminding us again that the entire book of Revelation is a vision of future events. As such, the revelator records what he saw in the vocabulary, language, and descriptive terms of his own time. What he actually means by "streets of gold" or "gates of pearl" may be beyond our wildest imagination or expectation. But that he sees a real place is obvious. He describes it as a city (Revelation 21:2). He speaks of its inhabitants (verse 24), its gates (verse 12), its size (verse 16), its foundations (verse 14), and its walls (verse 18). He describes the eternal state as a place of great activity, worship, and service to God. He also speaks of it as our eternal home, where we shall dwell forever.

While the number seven does not appear in these chapters, it is evident that the focus is on *seven "new" things* in the eternal state:

1. New heavens (21:1)

2. A new earth (21:1)

3. A new Jerusalem (21:2)

4. A new world order (21:5)

5. A new temple (21:22)

6. A new light (21:23)

7. A new paradise (22:1-5)

We are immediately swept up into the grandeur of this brand-new world. It is beyond anything of mere human imagination. In these two chapters we have the most detailed account in all the Bible of what heaven will be like. Here we find the redeemed of all time living in perfect peace and harmony in a final fixed moral state in which there is no sin, no rebellion, no pain, no sorrow, nor death.

The terms "new heaven" and "new earth" indicate a brand-new world is coming. *Heaven* (Greek, *ouranos)* refers to the atmospheric "heavens" (clouds, etc.), not to the dwelling place of God. It is the old planet and its atmosphere which have vanished and are replaced by a "new heaven and new earth." The heaven where God dwells is often called the "third heaven" (see 2 Corinthians 12:2) and needs no replacement. It is the place from which the new Jerusalem descends to earth.

The New Jerusalem

The hopes and dreams of the Jewish prophets looked forward to a new Jerusalem (see Isaiah 60; Ezekiel 40–48). If we are correct in dating the apocalypse at circa A.D. 95, the old Jerusalem would already have been in ashes for about 25 years. Therefore, it should not surprise us that John anticipated the arrival of a brand-new city "coming down from God" out of the third heaven. This event is mentioned three times in Revelation: 3:12; 21:2,10.

The new Jerusalem is referred to as "a bride adorned for her husband" (21:2 KJV). Later (21:9-10), John makes it clear that this is the bride of the Lamb, who was first introduced in Revelation 19:7-16. She returned from heaven with Christ and ruled with Him during the millennial kingdom. Now she assumes a new and permanent position as the "holy city."

This time she is called both the "bride" and "wife" of the Lamb (21:9). Yet she is also referred to as a "city." Robert Thomas comments, "The figure of a bride-city captures two characteristics of the new Jerusalem: God's personal relationship with His people (i.e., the bride) and the life of the people in communion with Him (i.e., the city)."[2]

A.T. Robertson points out that her "adornment" is from the Greek word from which we derive the term "cosmetics." The same term also applies to the adornment of the foundations of the city in Revelation 21:19-20."[3]

In anticipation of her arrival, a "great voice" speaks from heaven announcing that the "tabernacle of God is with men" (Revelation 21:3). This is a most dramatic announcement. It indicates that God is now accessible to His people. He is no longer on the distant throne of heaven. Nor is He hidden beyond the veil in the holy of holies. Rather:

1. God will dwell with us.

2. We shall be His people.

3. He will be our God.

4. God will wipe away our tears.

5. There shall be no more death.

6. There shall be no more sorrow.

7. There shall be no more pain.

The summary statement declares, "For the former things are passed away" (Revelation 21:4). Then God Himself, the One on the throne, said, "Behold, I make all things new" (verse 5). This one statement summarizes what the entire postscript is all about: "new things." This is not a repair job. Nor is it a major overhaul.

It is a brand-new creation. And the new Jerusalem is the apex of that creation.

In addition to telling us what will be in heaven, John also lists *seven things* that will *not* be in the eternal state:

1. Sea (Revelation 21:1)

2. Death (21:4)

3. Mourning (21:4)

4. Weeping (21:4)

5. Pain (21:4)

6. Curse (22:3)

7. Night (21:25)

Some have questioned the absence of the sea, but we must remember it was from the sea that the beast appeared in Revelation 13:1. Also, the absence of the sea indicates the eternal city is quite different from the natural world that now exists.

The picture painted in this chapter is that of the new Jerusalem suspended between heaven and earth. It is the final and permanent bond between the two. Notice also that the new earth, not just heaven, is a part of the final state. It would appear that the redeemed saints of God travel from heaven to earth by means of the levels of the eternal city.

The promise of God to the believers is that those who overcome (or persevere) will *"inherit all things"* (Revelation 21:7). This is the only reference to the believer's spiritual and eternal inheritance in the Revelation. But the concept is used frequently in the New Testament, especially by Jesus and Paul (see Matthew 5:5; 19:29; 25:34; Romans 4:13; 1 Corinthians 6:9). "All things" refers to all that is really essential and worthwhile for eternity. It is not a promise for earthly wealth and prosperity but for heavenly and eternal blessings. Paul had the same thing in mind when he wrote,

"And we know that all things work together for good to them that love God.... He that spared not his own Son, but delivered him up for us all, how shall he not with him also freely give us all things?" (Romans 8:28,32 KJV).

By contrast, the ungodly, unrepentant, and unbelieving multitudes, introduced by the adversative, "but," will never see the new Jerusalem. They will be cast into the lake of fire, which burns with fire and brimstone and is the "second death" (Revelation 21:8). There is no hope of a second chance mentioned. The *rejected* are listed in eight categories:

1. Fearful

2. Unbelieving

3. Abominable

4. Murderers

5. Whoremongers

6. Sorcerers

7. Idolaters

8. Liars

This is not to say that those who have ever committed these sins cannot be saved, but that those who continue to do so give evidence of an unrepentant and unconverted heart.

The Holy City

John was carried away "in the spirit" to a high mountain and shown the bride of Christ—the holy city of God. Beasley-Murray notes that "the Revelation as a whole may be characterized as *A Tale of Two Cities,* with the subtitle, 'The Harlot and the Bride.'"[4] With the collapse of Babylon, "the great harlot" (city of man), we were ushered into the millennium where Christ ruled in the earthly Jerusalem. Now we see the ultimate: the city of God, the bride of the lamb in all her eternal splendor and glory.

The most dominant characteristic of the holy city is the presence of the glory of God (Revelation 21:11). In the Old Testament, the *Shekinah* glory rested on the ark of the covenant in the holy of holies, but the prophet Ezekiel tells us that the glory departed before the final destruction of Solomon's Temple (see Ezekiel 8:4; 9:3; 10:4,18; 11:23). While the builders of the second temple prayed for the glory to return, there is no record that it ever did (Haggai 2:3). Israel's only hope in those dark days was that the glory would return one day (Haggai 2:7-9).

For more than 400 years the Temple was dark and empty. It stood as a gaunt symbol of Israel's empty ritual. No glory. No God. No power. It was not until Christ was born and the angels appeared and the "glory of the Lord shone round about them" that the glory returned (see Luke 2:9-14). The angels announced the birth of the Savior, Christ the Lord, and sang "Glory to God in the highest." In the person of Jesus Christ, the glory had finally returned. However, Israel officially rejected the Messiah, and the glory was made available to Gentiles who by faith received the Savior and became the temples of the Holy Spirit (see 1 Corinthians 6:19-20). In the meantime, Jerusalem was destroyed, and the second temple with it, by the Romans in A.D. 70. Even an attempt to rebuild a third temple during the tribulation period will not bring back the glory in itself.

The glory of God will, however, be in full expression in the new Jerusalem. The "glory" symbolizes God's presence with His people. The fact that He is there is far more significant than the dazzling description of the city itself. John MacArthur raises this same idea when he asks whether there is a temple in heaven. He notes that Revelation 11:19 refers to "the temple of God which is in heaven" (NASB), whereas, Revelation 21:22 says, "And I saw no temple therein: for the Lord God Almighty and the Lamb are its temple" (NASB). Rejecting the idea that there is presently a temple in heaven that will be removed in the future, MacArthur writes, "The temple in heaven is not a building: it is the Lord God Almighty Himself....In other words, the glory of God both illuminates heaven and defines it as a temple. One might say all heaven is the temple, and the glory and presence of the Lord permeate it."[5]

The *description of the city* by John the revelator is as follows:

1. *Splendor:* like a jasper, clear as crystal (Revelation 21:11)

2. *Wall:* 144 cubits (220 feet) high (verse 17)

3. *Gates:* giant pearls, named for the 12 tribes of Israel (verses 12, 21)

4. *Measurement:* foursquare—1,500-mile cube (verse 16)

5. *City itself:* pure gold, like clear glass (verse 18)

6. *Street:* pure gold, like transparent glass (verse 21)

7. *Temple:* God and the lamb are the temple (verse 22)

8. *Light:* glory of God and the lamb (verse 23)

9. *Nations:* those who are saved (verse 24)

10. *Access:* gates that are never closed (verse 25)

11. *Activity:* no night there (verse 25)

12. *Purity:* none who defile (verse 27)

A great deal has been written about whether this language is literal or symbolic or phenomenological. In truth, it combines all these elements. The whole book is filled with symbolic language; therefore, we cannot overlook certain obvious symbols here: twelve gates, twelve foundations, foursquare. It is also obvious that John is attempting to describe the indescribable. Human language, though inspired, is not fully adequate to describe the glories of the heavenly city. Thus, we read of "transparent gold" and "gates of pearl."

What is clear is that John is describing a real place where the saved, and only the saved, will dwell with God forever. The unsaved are excluded from this city totally and completely. Satan and those he has deceived are all in the lake of fire, from which there is no escape. The reference to "nations" and "kings" should not surprise us. Jesus promised that the gospel would be preached unto all nations (Matthew 24:14). John has earlier introduced us to those in heaven as "a great multitude ... of all nations" (Revelation 7:9). He has already referred to believers as "kings and priests" who reign with Christ (Revelation 5:10).

The importance of our relationship to Christ is emphasized again in the last verse of the chapter (21:27). Only those whose names are written in the Lamb's book of life can live in the holy city. This includes all the redeemed of all time: Old Testament saints, the New Testament church, tribulation saints, and millennial saints. Thus, we see the perfect blending of the redeemed in the holy city in that the twelve gates are named for the twelve tribes of Israel and the twelve foundations for the twelve apostles.

The picture of our glorious future with Christ is that of our eternal reign with Him. The glorified saints of God will reign with Christ forever. The final vision of biblical prophecy (Revelation 21–22) reveals the redeemed in a state of eternal glory reigning with Christ.

Paradise Regained

In the final chapter of Revelation, we learn that all that was lost in the beginning will finally be regained. Paradise is restored in the holy city. The biblical story, which began in the garden, ends in the eternal city. In between, there stands the cross of Jesus Christ, which changed the destiny of mankind forever. Revelation

22 clearly indicates that the eternal state will return the new creation to the inherent qualities of the Garden of Eden—only on a grander scale. Then, and only then, will the Creator's true intention for humanity finally be realized.

The *river of life* is reminiscent of the river of Eden, whose tributaries flowed in four directions (Genesis 2:10,14). The metaphoric use of a river of spiritual refreshment can be found throughout the Old Testament (Psalm 36:9; Proverbs 10:11; 13:14; Isaiah 12:3; Jeremiah 2:13; 17:13; Ezekiel 47:9; Zechariah 14:8). The beautiful picture that is painted by the words of this prophecy reminds us that the best of the natural world will be preserved in the eternal world.

The *tree of life* is presented in Genesis 2:9 as a single tree. In Ezekiel's millennial vision, he sees several trees on both sides of the great river (Ezekiel 47:12). But the Revelation record reconnects us with the Genesis record. In both accounts, this tree is a singular tree. Here, in Revelation 22:2, it bears twelve types of fruit—one for each month of the year. Thus, it is perpetually in bloom. There is no winter season in the eternal state.

The reference to using the leaves for "healing" (Greek, *therapeian*) derives from the term *therapeutic*. John Walvoord notes that the root meaning of the term conveys the idea of "health-giving."[6] There is no need of healing from sickness or disease since the consequences of sin have been removed and the "former things are passed away" (21:4 KJV). Thus, the tree and its leaves are seen as a source of life and health in the eternal state.

The ultimate proof that this indeed is a return to Edenic conditions is the removal of the *divine curse* (Revelation 22:3). This curse was first pronounced against the participants in the first act of rebellion in Genesis 3:14-19). The actual objects of the curse were Satan and the earth ("ground") itself. But the implications of the curse affected all involved:

1. *Serpent*—cursed above all animals

2. *Woman*—sorrow and pain in childbirth

3. *Man*—"Cursed is the ground for your sake"

The Old Testament record of man's rebellion against God begins and ends with a curse. The sin of Adam and Eve is cursed, and its consequences are severe (Genesis 3:14-19). Even in the Law of Moses, there is the threat of the curse for those who break the law (Deuteronomy 27:13-26). The Old Testament ends with the threat of a curse: "lest I come and smite the earth with a curse" (Malachi 4:6).

The Old Testament begins so well ("in the beginning God") and ends so badly ("with a curse"). It starts with all the glorious potential of the divine creation and ends with the threat of divine judgment. It opens in paradise and closes with mankind lost in sin's condemnation. How different the New Testament! It opens with Jesus Christ (Matthew 1:1), and it closes with Jesus Christ (Revelation 22:22). It begins with His first coming and concludes with His second coming.

God Is There!

The removal of the divine curse makes access to God a reality in the new paradise. We are no longer barred from His presence. The throne of God has come to earth and is the central feature of the eternal city. It is the throne of God and the Lamb, who rule jointly over the eternal state. We who believe in Jesus Christ know that He and the Father are one. We believe in Him even though we have never seen Him. But in the eternal city, faith shall become sight—we shall see his face (Revelation 22:4).

The Lord God is all the light we will ever need. Because of God's presence, three things will *not* be found in the new paradise: 1) No night; 2) No candle; and 3) No sun. God will outshine all other light sources because He is the source of light. Every student of the Bible must remember that God Himself is the ultimate focus of biblical prophecy. It all points to our ultimate consummation and fulfillment in Him.

We who are seated positionally with Christ in "heavenly places" are destined for the throne as joint heirs with Him (Ephesians 1:30; 2:6). In eternity we will continue to reign with Christ "when he hands over the kingdom to God the Father" (1 Corinthians 15:24). Thus, the millennial kingdom will be merged into the eternal kingdom of God forever.

All of us are curious about the future. There is something in human nature that wants to know what is going to happen next. God speaks to that need by revealing the future before it happens. Hundreds of biblical prophecies continue to give us a picture of the world to come. And that world is one where God is all we will ever need for all eternity.

If we really believe that Jesus Christ is coming again to rapture the church, judge the world, set up his kingdom, and rule for all eternity, then we ought to live like it! Many Christians lose sight of their eternal destiny. They become bogged down with the mundane problems of life and allow themselves to become worried, depressed, angry, or confused. Why? Because they forget what their final destiny is really all about.

If we really kept our perspective on eternity, we would not let the problems of earth get us down. But the temptation to focus on the temporal, instead of the eternal, is a constant struggle for all of us. Whether our daily problems revolve around our health, finances, family, friends, career, or temporal security, true Christians must look beyond all of these things to the only real source of security in our lives—Jesus Christ!

What Can We Do in the Meantime?

The timing of the last days is in God's hands. From a human standpoint it appears that we are standing on the threshold of the final frontier. The pieces of the puzzle are all in place. As the sands of time slip through the hourglass of eternity, we are all moving closer to an appointment with destiny. The only question is, "How much time is left?"

The tension between living for today and looking for tomorrow is one of the realities of the Christian life. We often find ourselves caught between the here-and-now and the here-after. On the one hand, we need to be ready for Jesus to come at any moment. On the other hand, we have God-given responsibilities to fulfill in this world in the meantime.

We are living in a time of great crisis, but it is also a time of great opportunity. We must be prepared for the challenges that lie ahead of us. New technologies will make our lives more convenient, but they will also make us more dependent on those conveniences. Medical advancements will continue to pose enormous challenges in the area of biomedical ethics. The shifting sands of sociopolitical change will also challenge our national and international policies in the days ahead. We will find ourselves living in a very different world from the one into which we were born. All of these changes and challenges will confront us in the days ahead.

Preparing for Christ's return is something each one of us must do for ourselves. No one else can get our hearts ready to meet God. You and I must do that ourselves. Jesus urges us to do three things in view of His second coming:

1. Keep watching (Matthew 24:42).

2. Be ready (Matthew 24:44).

3. Keep serving (Matthew 24:46).

Erwin Lutzer, the senior pastor of Moody Church in Chicago, has reminded us there are "five unshakable pillars" to enable us to withstand the onslaught of secularism in our society today:[1]

1. *God still reigns.*

Human leaders will come and go. Some will be better, some worse. Some will be what we deserve—a reflection of our own weakness and sinfulness. But behind the scene of human governments, God still reigns over the eternal destiny of mankind. Beyond this temporal world, God rules from the throne in heaven. He guides His children and overrules in the affairs of men and nations to accomplish His will and purposes. The Bible assures us "there is no authority except that which God has established" (Romans 13:1). Regardless of who our leaders are, we are to offer "prayers, intercession and thanksgiving...for kings and those in authority" (1 Timothy 2:1-2).

2. *The church is still precious.*

During this present age, God is still working through His church to evangelize the world. Jesus gave us clear direction about what we are to be doing until He returns. He said: "Go and make disciples of all nations, baptizing them in the name of the Father and of the Son and of the Holy Spirit, and teaching them to obey everything I have commanded you ... to the very end of the age" (Matthew 28:19-20). The church may flourish or be persecuted in the days ahead, but she is to be faithful to her mission until Jesus calls her home to glory (1 Thessalonians 4:13-17).

3. *Our mission is still clear.*

The church stands as the salt and light of God in society. We are to "declare the praises of him who called you out of darkness into his wonderful light" (1 Peter 2:9). Lutzer suggests that we can accomplish this by: 1) Representing Christ to the world by a godly lifestyle; 2) winning people to Christ through intellectual and moral confrontation with a loving persuasiveness; and 3) strengthening our families as a testimony to God's grace. The integrity of sincere and authentic Christian lives and families speaks volumes to a lost world that is desperate for meaning and purpose. We cannot underestimate the spiritual impact that true Christianity has on those who have no answers to the overwhelming problems of life. Bill Hybles has said: "When Christians live out their faith with authenticity and boldness ... they create quite a stir just being themselves."[2]

4. *Our focus is still heaven.*

It is easy for modern American Christians to forget that heaven is our real destiny. So many believers today live in such peace and affluence that they forget about heaven. We actually think that God's purpose is to bless our lives here on earth. Dave

Hunt has observed: "Unfortunately, too many persons—even dedicated Christians—find heaven a topic of only minor interest because they consider it irrelevant to the challenges of this present life."[3] We must remember, however, that this world is no friend to grace. As time passes, we should expect a continual moral decline in secular society. The Bible reminds us that there will be an "increase of wickedness" and that "terrible times" will come in the last days (Matthew 24:12; 2 Timothy 3:1). In the meantime, whatever success we have in this world must be measured in the light of our eternal destiny. Joe Stowell reminds us that if we make heaven our primary point of reference it will transform our relationship to everything that is temporal in this world.[4] C.S. Lewis wrote: "Christians who did most for the present world were just those who thought most of the next."[5]

5. *Our victory is still certain.*

The ultimate Bible prophecies focus on the triumph of Christ and His bride—the church (Revelation 19). They assure us that we will share in His victorious reign. Whatever transpires in the meantime must be viewed in light of our eternal destiny. Peter Marshall, former chaplain of the U.S. Senate, said: "It is better to fail at a cause that will ultimately succeed than to succeed in a cause that will ultimately fail."[6] Until the trumpet sounds and the Lord calls us home, we have the Great Commission to fulfill and the world to evangelize. There is no reason to let up now. Since we have no clear date for the termination of the present age, we must keep on serving Christ until He comes.

A young African martyr wrote these words in his prison cell before he died:

> I'm part of the fellowship of the unashamed, the die has been cast, I have stepped over the line, the decision has

been made—I'm a disciple of Jesus Christ—I won't look back, let up, slow down, back away or be still.

My past is redeemed, my present makes sense, my future is secure—I'm finished and done with low living, sight walking, smooth knees, colorless dreams, tamed visions, worldly talking, cheap giving and dwarfed goals.

My face is set, my gait is fast, my goal is heaven, my road is narrow, my way is rough, my companions are few, my guide is reliable, my mission is clear. I won't give up, shut up, let up until I have stayed up, stored up, prayed up for the cause of Jesus Christ.

I must go till He comes, give till I drop, preach till everyone knows, work till He stops me and when He comes for His own, He will have no trouble recognizing me because my banner will have been clear.[7]

What Should We Be Doing?

Since we can never be sure when God's purposes for His church will be finalized, we must remain obedient to our Lord's commands regarding His church. This was made clear to the disciples at the time of Christ's ascension to heaven. They had asked if He was going to restore the kingdom to Israel at that time, and Jesus told them, "It is not for you to know the times or dates the Father has set by His own authority" (Acts 1:7). Two facts are clear in this statement: 1) The date has been set; and 2) we aren't supposed to know it because we have a responsibility to fulfill in the meantime.

In the very next verse, Jesus gave the Great Commission, telling the disciples they would be empowered by the Holy Spirit to be His witnesses in Jerusalem, Judea, Samaria, and "to the ends of the earth" (Acts 1:8). Then, to their amazement, He ascended into heaven, leaving them gazing intently into the sky. Two men in white (probably angels) appeared and asked, "Why do you stand here looking into the sky? This same Jesus, who has been taken from you into heaven, will come back in the same way you have seen him go into heaven" (Acts 1:11).

All too often, today's Christians are just like those early disciples. We spend more time gazing into the sky and speculating about Christ's return than we do serving Him. The angels' point was to remind the disciples that His return is certain. Thus we shouldn't waste time and energy worrying about when or whether Christ will return. Believe that He is coming again on schedule and be about His business in the meantime.

Jesus left several instructions about what we ought to be doing while we await His coming:

1. *Witness for Him everywhere you go.* Our Lord told His disciples to be His witnesses everywhere—even to the farthest ends of the earth (Acts 1:8).

2. *"Go into all the world and preach the good news"* (Mark 16:15). This command emphasizes the evangelistic and missionary nature of the church's ministry during the present era. We are to take the gospel to the whole world.

3. *"Repentance and forgiveness of sins will be preached… to all nations"* our Lord declared in Luke 24:47. Calling men and women to repent and believe the gospel is the twofold nature of the evangelistic enterprise.

4. *"Make disciples of all nations, baptizing them,"* Jesus said in Matthew 28:19. Making converts and discipling them in their walk with God is a major emphasis of the church's mission.

5. *Build the church, in every generation.* Jesus told His disciples that He would build His church with such power that "the gates of hell shall not prevail against it" (Matthew 16:18 KJV). Jesus pictured the church being on the march until He calls her home.

6. *"Work… until I come back"* (Luke 19:13), Jesus said in the parable of the talents. In this parable, the servants were to "put this money to work" until their master returned. We are to stay busy about the Master's business until He returns.

7. *Remain faithful until He returns.* Our Lord concluded His prophetic message in the Olivet Discourse by reminding His disciples to continue in faithful and wise service even though He might be gone a long time (Matthew 24:45; 25:14-21).

Is There Any Hope for Our Generation?

Genuine spiritual revival is the result of the outpouring of the Holy Spirit on the church. Throughout history, God often has moved to bless His people in a fresh and powerful way. Genuine revival came as God's people were convicted of their sin, repented and gained a new zeal and devotion for God in their lives. In revival, the self-centered, half-hearted indifference that so often dominates our lives is swept aside by a new and genuine desire to live for God.

Revival begins to renew our values and redirect our lives. It calls us to a more serious walk with Christ, and results in substantial and abiding fruit (see John 15:16; Galatians 5:22-23). The changes that occur, both in individual believers and in the church collectively, speak convincingly to the world about what it really means to belong to Christ. Such revival comes when God's people pray, when God's truth is proclaimed, and when God's Spirit moves in our lives.

Unfortunately, there is little evidence of genuine revival today. Some have lost hope of it altogether. Others have diluted the gospel message in order to make its appeal more acceptable to today's generation. Evangelist Bailey Smith has correctly observed: "The Christ of the Bible has been reduced to a fallible humanitarian. Salvation has been repackaged into a feel-good experience. Forgotten in today's 'gospel revisionism' is the message that sent Christ to the cross and the disciples to martyrdom. Today's gospel 'lite' is hardly worth living for and certainly not worth dying for."[8]

If we are going to make an impact on our generation for the cause of Christ, it must be soon. Since we have no idea how much time is left, we dare not let the time slip away indiscriminately. If we are going to use wisely whatever time God gives us, we must be about His business with a sense of urgency. On the one hand, we dare not *presume* on God's grace by assuming we have plenty of time left to get the job done. On the other hand, we dare not *terminate* the grace of God by assuming it is too late for our generation.

Prophecy lovers are especially prone to this second reaction. We are eschatological pessimists. We know all too well that things are going to get worse, not better. We believe that a growing religious apostasy is strangling the spiritual life out of our churches. And we have little hope in human efforts to revitalize our dying culture. Therefore, it is easy for us to give up and quit trying to reach our generation with the gospel.

This is the downside to the pretribulational position. It *can* (not must) lead to a kind of eschatological "fatalism." If we are not careful, we can abandon our calling and just sit and wait for the rapture. But there is no biblical warrant for such fatalism. The Bible never tells us that things will be so bad that we should give up and quit preaching altogether and wait for "the end." Rather, the Bible clearly instructs us to keep preaching, testifying and witnessing, knowing that Christ will continue to build His church until He comes (Matthew 16:18).

In the meantime, we can live with our eyes on the skies— watching for Christ to come—and with our feet on the earth, working for Him until He comes. This balance of *expectation* (that

Jesus could come at any moment) and *participation* (serving Him faithfully until He comes) is what the Christian life is really all about. Living in the light of His coming keeps us focused on what is really important in life. It also keeps our attention on the balance between our present responsibilities and our future expectations.

The hope of the second coming is the strongest encouragement for us to live right until Jesus comes. The ultimate incentive to right living is the fact that we will face our Lord when He returns. Each of us needs to be ready when that day comes. If we live out faithfully whatever time is left to us, we will surely hear Him say, "Well done, good and faithful servant!"

The Outcome
Is Certain!

The world is speeding toward its ultimate date with destiny. Every day that passes moves us closer to the end. The people and the planet have a divine appointment to keep. As the clock of time ticks away, mankind comes closer and closer to earth's final hour.

It is only a matter of time until our planet will be plunged into the most devastating catastrophe imaginable. The outcome is certain. Global conflagration is clearly predicted in biblical prophecy. The only real question is: How much time is left?

Almost 2,000 years ago, the apostle Peter said, "The end of all things is near. Therefore be clear minded and self-controlled so that you can pray" (1 Peter 4:7). Way back in the New Testament era, Peter and the other apostles sensed that they had moved dramatically closer to the consummation of God's plan for this world. The Old Testament Age had come to an end, and they were now part of a new era.

Peter's reference to the end is expressed by a perfect-tense verb in the original Greek text. This means the action involved is a present reality with future consequences. It could just as appropriately be translated, "The end of all things has already begun." For Peter, the end of the age was already a present reality.

The first coming of Christ initiated the end of the age (see Acts 2:14-20; Hebrews 1:2), and His second coming will terminate the end of the age (Matthew 24:30). Therefore, the entire Church Age is a "last days" in a general sense. And the very end of those days is a specific "last days," or a "last of the last days."

Scripture also speaks of the end as a future event. The apostle Paul predicted, "There will be terrible times in the last days" (2 Timothy 3:1). The opening verse of the apocalypse refers to "things which must shortly come to pass" (Revelation 1:1 KJV) and goes on to warn us that "the time is near" (Revelation 1:3). Scripture also presents Christ's coming as an imminent reality. "Behold, I am coming soon!" Christ promised (Revelation 22:7). He will come suddenly, and He could come at any moment.

That leaves us asking this question: What time is it now? Peter referred to the *present*, saying, "[Christ] was revealed in these last times" (1 Peter 1:20). At the same time, Peter referred to the coming of Christ as a future event, "ready to be revealed in the last time" (1 Peter 1:5). It is clear that he viewed the last times as both a present reality and a future event.

The Bible affirms three basic facts about the coming of Christ and the end of the age.

First, *we are living in the last days.* Every generation of Christians has lived with the hope of the imminent return of Christ. We believe that He could return at any moment. There is no prophetic event that remains to be fulfilled before the way can be opened for Him to return. In fact, certain events, like the return of Israel to her land, indicate that we are close to the end.

Second, ***God's timetable is not our timetable.*** Peter himself told us that "in the last days scoffers will come," questioning the promise of His second coming (2 Peter 3:3-4). They will reject the idea of God's intervention in human history and suggest that all things are moving forward at their own pace without God. These skeptics will also fail to anticipate God's coming judgment upon the world (2 Peter 3:8). God's perspective is not limited to human time. But we dare not mistake the patience of God for a change in His plans. He is waiting, giving His people time to repent. The Bible warns: "He who is coming will come and will not delay" (Hebrews 10:37).

Third, ***Christ's coming is always growing closer.*** The Bible emphatically promises that Christ is coming again (Luke 12:40; Philippians 3:20; Titus 2:13; Hebrews 9:28). Scripture urges us to be watching, waiting, and ready for our Lord to return. Every day that passes brings us one day closer. Whether He returns next week or 1,000 years from now, we are to be living as though He were coming today.

Looking Ahead

Anticipation is the key to preparation. If you were expecting an important visitor, you would probably keep looking for him to arrive. Chances are that you would also make proper preparation for his visit. Your anticipation of the visitor's arrival would influence your preparation for his visit. The same is true of our anticipation of the coming of Christ. If we really believe He is coming, we will want to be prepared for Him when He comes.

Jesus illustrated this in His own prophetic teaching with the story of the ten virgins (Matthew 25:1-13). Only those who were prepared for the wedding were invited into the wedding banquet. The others were left out. Jesus used this illustration to remind us to "keep watch" because we don't know the time of His coming.

Dr. John Walvoord comments on this passage, saying: "The important point here ... is that preparation should precede the second coming of Christ and that it will be too late when He comes."[1]

If we can take seriously the biblical predictions about the end times, then we must make preparation now for what is coming in the future. We cannot wait until all other options have been exhausted. The time for action is now. If you are not sure about your own relationship with Christ, make sure before it is too late.

There are many things that demand our attention in life. There are many voices calling to us, and many images that flash across our minds. But no matter what our focus in life, one thing is certain: All of us will face death at some point. We cannot avoid it. All of us are vulnerable.

Death is the great equalizer. It makes no difference how rich or poor, famous or infamous, respected or rejected you may have been in this life. When you face death you are facing an impartial judge. The Bible reminds us that "all have sinned" (Romans 3:23) and the "wages of sin is death" (Romans 6:23). When death comes knocking at your door, all that really matters is that you are ready to face it.

The reason Jesus came the first time was to die for our sins. He came to pay the price for our sins so that we might be forgiven. He is called our Redeemer because He has redeemed us from God's judgment against our sin. The apostle Peter wrote: "You were redeemed ... with the precious blood of Christ.... He was chosen before the creation of the world, but was revealed in these last times for your sake" (1 Peter 1:18-20).

What Does the Future Hold?

The Bible predicts the major events of the future. It gives us the "big picture" of what is coming in the end times. The specific details are not always as clear, and we must be cautious about trying to speculate beyond what the Bible itself actually says. Our goal ought to be one of balance. Don't *minimize* or *maximize* the future. Don't make the Bible say *less* than it is saying, but also don't try to make it say *more* than it is saying.

The question of the interpretation of biblical prophecy always raises the issue of one's eschatological view. Those who prefer a literal interpretation of prophecy foresee Israel back in the land, the probable rebuilding of the Temple, the rise of a literal antichrist, the making and breaking of a real peace treaty, and the ultimate invasion of Israel, leading to the battle of Armageddon.

We do not believe that we can simply "spiritualize" away the basic statements of Bible prophecy. For us, the rapture means being "caught up" into heaven (1 Thessalonians 4:13-17) and the "one thousand years" of Christ's reign means 1,000 years (Revelation 20:4). We do not discount the use of figurative or symbolic language in prophetic passages (e.g., the Lamb, the beast, the dragon). But we believe strongly that prophetic passages pointing to the second coming of Christ refer to specific people and events, as did the prophetic passages pointing to His first coming (e.g., Isaiah 53).

Based on a pretribulational viewpoint, we believe that Jesus Christ will return to rapture the church prior to the tribulation period. In commenting on this spectacular event, the apostle Paul wrote: "For the Lord himself will come down from heaven, with a loud command, with the voice of the archangel and with the trumpet call of God, and the dead in Christ will rise first. After that, we who are still alive and are left will be caught up (Greek *harpazō*, "snatched away") with them in the clouds to meet the Lord in the air. And so we will be with the Lord forever" (1 Thessalonians 4:16-17).

The general picture of the future in biblical prophecy centers around 15 key predictions:

1. *Spread of the gospel message and the growth of the church.*

Jesus established the church and promised to continue to build it until He returns (Matthew 16:18). He also predicted that the gospel "will be preached in the whole world as a testimony to all nations" (Matthew 24:14). The growth of the church and world evangelism will continue until the body of Christ is complete. There is no specific prediction of how long the Church Age will last. It will continue until the Lord returns to call the church home.

2. *Increase of wickedness and the spread of evil.*

The Bible also predicts that the "increase of evil" will continue until the end of the age (Matthew 24:12). Paul predicted that "there will be terrible times in the last days" and then defined those days as a time of unparalleled greed, avarice and selfishness (2 Timothy 3:1-5). Today, these prophecies are being fulfilled at a startling pace.

3. *Rise of false prophets and apostate religion.*

Jesus Himself warned about the coming of "false Christs" and "false prophets" (Matthew 24:4,24). Peter predicted: "there will be false teachers" (2 Peter 2:1). Paul called them "false apostles, deceitful workmen, masquerading as apostles of Christ" (2 Corinthians 11:13). The Bible seems to indicate that false prophets and apostate religion will become worse as we get closer to the end (Jude 17-18).

4. *Return of Israel to the Promised Land.*

"I will bring you from the nations ... where you have been scattered," wrote the prophet (Ezekiel 20:34). "I will bring your children ... from the ends of the earth," promised Isaiah (43:5-6). In 1948, these ancient prophecies were fulfilled when Israel became a nation again after nearly 1,900 years in exile. Ezekiel predicted a two-stage return: 1) Physical regathering; and 2) Spiritual rebirth (Ezekiel 37:1-14).

5. *Conflict in the Middle East.*

The general picture of the future is one of turmoil between the Jews and the Arabs in the Middle East. Jesus warned that there would continually be "wars and rumors of wars" in the future (Matthew 24:6-7). The prophet Joel predicts the nations invading Israel in the last days—"multitudes, multitudes in the valley of decision: for the day of the Lord is near in the valley of decision" (Joel 3:2-14 KJV). Ezekiel (38:1-6) predicts a massive invasion of Israel in the "latter days" by a coalition of nations—Magog, Persia, Libya, Ethiopia, Gomer and Togarmah. Collectively, the prophets foresee Israel back in the land but under constant threat of attack.

6. *The rapture of the church.*

At some undated time in the future, Jesus will return to rapture the church (believers) to heaven. When He was preparing to return to heaven, Jesus promised, "I will come back and take you to be with me" (John 14:3). Paul predicted that those who had died in Christ "will rise first," then the living believers "will be caught up" into the clouds and united with those who have been resurrected (1 Thessalonians 4:13-17). The rapture will happen "in a flash, in the twinkling of an eye, at the last trumpet" (1 Corinthians 15:51). The rapture precedes the tribulation period and fulfills the Lord's promise: "I will keep you from the hour of trial that is going to come upon the whole world" (Revelation 3:10).

7. *Marriage of Christ and the church in heaven.*

After the rapture and prior to the return of Christ to the earth, the "wedding of the Lamb" will take place in heaven (Revelation

19:7-9). The marriage is followed by the "wedding supper" (the reception) and appears to last for seven years during the tribulation period. Christ is pictured as the husband or bridegroom, and the church is pictured as the bride of Christ (see Ephesians 5:25-27; 2 Corinthians 11:2). Following the pattern of traditional Jewish weddings in biblical times, Jesus pictured the promised engagement, followed by the departure of the groom to prepare a place for the bride, followed by the groom's sudden return at "midnight" to call the bride away (Matthew 25:1-6).

8. *Rise of the antichrist and the false prophet.*

Paul predicts the rise of the "lawless one" after the restrainer (indwelling Spirit in the church) has been removed (2 Thessalonians 2:3-8). "Then the lawless one will be revealed," Paul writes. This seems to indicate that the identity of the antichrist will remain a mystery until after the rapture. John calls him "the beast" in Revelation 13:1-10, and "the antichrist" in 1 John 2:22. John also pictures this last great political leader being assisted by the "false prophet"—a false religious leader (Revelation 13:11-18). Together, they deceive the whole world during the tribulation period.

9. *Development of a global system.*

The book of Revelation clearly predicts the world of the future will combine a global economy (Revelation13:16-17) with a world government (13:8; 17:1-18) and a world religion (13:8-12). The global economy is already a reality! The world government is already in the process of forming under the banner of democracy. At the present time, the United States is the major player in the attempt to insure global peace and security. While there is no real consensus of world religion today, such could easily happen after the rapture. In the meantime, the sentiment of apostate Christendom continues to favor a religion of universal tolerance.

10. *The tribulation period.*

Despite efforts at world peace, the rule of the antichrist will be marked by wars of mass destruction, environmental disasters and divine judgments (Revelation 6:1-16; 9:16-18). Daniel (12:1) calls this period a "time of distress." Zephaniah (1:14) calls it the "great day of the Lord." Jeremiah (30:7) calls it "a time of trouble for Jacob." John calls it the "wrath of the Lamb" (Revelation 16:16). Most pretribulationalists view the tribulation period as being simultaneous with the seven years of Daniel's seventieth week (Daniel 9:24-27). We believe the antichrist will make a peace treaty with Israel during this period only to break the treaty at the midpoint of the tribulation period (Daniel 9:27).

11. *The battle of Armageddon.*

The prophetic picture indicates a series of wars of mass destruction are coming in the future (Revelation 6-18). These will result in nearly half the population of the world being destroyed (Revelation 8:7; 9:16-18). Eventually, these wars will culminate in a final battle at "the place … called Armageddon" (Revelation 16:16). The mountains will be "soaked with blood" (Isaiah 34:3). "All the nations that fought against Jerusalem" will be destroyed (Zechariah 14:12-13). In the end, Christ Himself will return and conquer the beast and the false prophet, casting them into the lake of fire (Revelation 19:11-20). Satan will be bound in the abyss for a thousand years (Revelation 20:1-2). The greatest battle in the history of the world will be won when Jesus conquers the enemies of God by the power of His spoken word (Revelation 19:15,21).

12. *Triumphal return of Christ.*

Jesus predicted that one day "the sign of the Son of Man will appear in the sky.... They will see the Son of Man coming on the clouds of the sky, with power and great glory" (Matthew 24:30). Zechariah (14:3-4) predicted that "his feet will stand on the Mount of Olives" and it will "split in two" when He returns. Isaiah (63:1-4) pictures Christ marching in triumph in blood-splattered garments on the "day of vengeance." Revelation 19:11-16 describes Him coming on a white horse with the church, robed in white, at His side. He "judges" with eyes of "blazing fire" and "makes war" with the "sharp sword" of His spoken word. He treads the "winepress... of the wrath of God" when He comes to rule as "King of kings and Lord of lords."

13. *Millennial kingdom.*

The Old Testament prophets pictured the coming Messianic Age as a time of peace and prosperity for Israel when "they will beat their swords into plowshares" and "nation will not take up sword against nation" (Isaiah 2:2-4). They also foresaw the Messiah reigning "on David's throne and over his kingdom" (Isaiah 9:6-7). The New Testament pictures this as a time when Christ rules on earth with His bride, the church, for 1,000 years (Revelation 20:1-6). During this time we will "reign on the earth" as kings and priests with Christ (Revelation 5:10). Those who have survived the tribulation will live on into the millennial kingdom as life continues on earth for 1,000 years.

14. *Great white throne judgment.*

After the 1,000-year reign, Satan will be loosed from the abyss and attempt one last time to overthrow the kingdom of God (Revelation 20:7-10). This time he will be permanently defeated and cast into the lake of fire. The millennial kingdom will be transferred into the eternal kingdom of God (1 Corinthians 15:24), and the great white throne judgment settles the eternal condemnation of all the lost of all time whose names are "not found written in the book of life"(Revelation 20:11-15). At that time, even "death and hell" will be thrown into the lake of fire that is the "second death."

15. *Eternity.*

The Bible pictures the eternal state as one of perpetual bliss where paradise is regained. The "tree of life" is restored (Revelation 22:2) and the redeemed of all time live together in the "new heavens" and "new earth" with the "new Jerusalem" as their central dwelling place (Revelation 21:1-23). Tears are wiped away and there will be "no more death or mourning or crying or pain" (Revelation 21:41). Isaiah (65:19) predicted, "the sound of weeping and crying will be heard no more." God the Father and Christ the Lamb are pictured as the light and the temple of the eternal city (Revelation 21:22-23). The twelve gates of the city are named for the twelve tribes of Israel and the twelve foundations for the twelve apostles, emphasizing the eternal unity of the redeemed people of God (Revelation 21:11-14).

Jesus said: "I am the resurrection and the life. He who believes in me will live, even though he dies" (John 11:25). This is the great promise of Christ. He calls us to faith in Him and then promises to reward us with eternal life (John 3:16; 4:36; 5:24). The Bible pictures eternity as a place of great activity as we serve Christ forever. In the meantime, we are "pilgrims" passing through the temporary domain of earth on our way to our ultimate home. Joe Stowell writes: "To claim the pilgrim's identity means that we always know we're not home yet. For us, the best is yet to come."[2]

Until the trumpet sounds, or death comes to usher us into eternity, we are to keep our eyes on the Savior (Hebrews 12:2). He is the focus of Bible prophecy. The prophets predicted His first coming with incredible accuracy, and they have done the same for His second coming. Jesus said: "When these things begin to take place, stand up and lift up your heads, because your redemption is drawing near" (Luke 21:28).

Whatever else is coming in the future, we can rest assured that Jesus is coming again!

Notes

CHAPTER 1

1. See Bill Bright and J.N. Damoose, *Red Sky in the Morning* (Orlando: New Life Publications, 1998); Charles Colson, *Against the Night* (Ann Arbor, MI: Servant Publications, 1989); John Hagee, *Final Dawn Over Jerusalem* (Nashville: Thomas Nelson, 1998).

2. Cf. Gary DeMar, *Last Days Madness* (Brentwood, TN: Wolgemuth & Hyatt, 1991); R.C. Sproul, *The Last Days According to Jesus* (Grand Rapids, MI: Baker, 1998); Jerry Newcombe, *Coming Again* (Colorado Springs: Chariot Victor, 1999).

3. Cf. examples in Alva McClain, *The Greatness of the Kingdom* (Chicago: Moody Press, 1968), pp. 462-63.

4. John F. Walvoord, quoted by Randall Price, "Toward 2000: Discerning the Signs of the Times," in *World of the Bible News & Views* (March 1999), p. 1.

5. Ibid.

6. This is emphasized by Arnold Fruchtenbaum, *The Footsteps of the Messiah* (Tustin, CA: Ariel Press, 1982). Cf. also Tim LaHaye, *Understanding the Last Days* (Eugene, OR: Harvest House, 1998).

7. Price, op. cit., p. 1.

8. Ibid.

9. Cf. various examples in DeMar, Sproul and Newcombe.

10. Cf. various references in Russell Chandler, *Doomsday* (Ann Arbor, MI: Servant Publications, 1993), pp. 245-58; Marvin Pate and Calvin Haines, *Doomsday Delusions* (Downers Grove, IL: InterVarsity Press, 1995), pp. 133-47.

11. Mark Noll, "Misreading the Signs of the Times," *Christianity Today* (February 6, 1987), pp. 10-11.

12. Richard Kyle, *The Last Days Are Here Again* (Grand Rapids, MI: Baker, 1998), pp. 121-22.

13. B.J. Oropeza, *99 Reasons Why No One Knows When Christ Will Return* (Downers Grove, IL: InterVarsity Press, 1994), p. 34.

14. R.A. Torrey, *The Return of the Lord Jesus* (Los Angeles: Bible Institute of Los Angeles, 1913), p. 89.

15. Kyle, p. 107.

16. Ibid., p. 113.

17. Richard Mouw, "What the Old Dispensationalists Taught Me," *Christianity Today* (March 6, 1995), p. 34.

CHAPTER 2

1. Tertullian, quoted by I.D.E. Thomas, *Golden Treasury of Patristic Quotations* (Oklahoma City, OK: Hearthstone Publications, 1996), p. 215.

2. Ibid., p. 90.

3. David Reagan, "The Certainty of the Lord's Coming Reign," in *The Lamplighter* (February 1999), pp. 6-8.

4. David Larsen, *Jews, Gentiles and the Church* (Grand Rapids, MI: Discovery House, 1995), pp. 310, 311.

5. Thomas Ice and Timothy Demy, *The Truth About the Millennium* (Eugene, OR: Harvest House, 1996), p. 8.

6. John Walvoord, *Prophecy* (Nashville: Thomas Nelson, 1993), p. 139.

7. David Reagan, "Recognizing the Signs of the Times," in *The Lamplighter* (June 1998).

8. Ibid. Cf. also Gary Frazier, *Seven Signs of the Second Coming of Christ* (Arlington, TX: Discovery Ministries, 1998).

9. Stanley Ellisen, "The Prophets Promised His Coming," in *10 Reasons Why Jesus Is Coming Soon* (Sisters, OR: Multnomah Press, 1998), p. 75.

10. For a detailed discussion, see Edward E. Hindson, *The Puritans' Use of Scripture in the Development of an Apocalyptical Hermeneutic* (Pretoria: University of South Africa, 1984), pp. 14-19. The Talmud ascribes this to *Tanna debe Eliyahu* ("the School of Elijah"). This non-canonical source was quoted widely by Bede, Isidore of Seville, and even Martin Luther. Cf. C.A. Patrides, *The Grand Design of God: The Literary Form of the Christian View of History* (Princeton: Princeton University Press, 1977). For a brief summary, see Hindson, "Medieval and Reformation Backgrounds of Dispensationalism," in *Conservative Theological Journal*, 1, 3 (December 1997), pp. 190-202.

11. See "Uh-Oh, Maybe We Missed the Big Day," *Newsweek* (August 11, 1997), p. 15. Cf. also, Harold Hoehner, *Chronological Aspects of the Life of Christ* (Grand Rapids, MI: Zondervan, 1977), pp. 11-25.

12. Cf. Thomas Ice and Randall Price, *Ready to Rebuild* (Eugene, OR: Harvest House, 1992).

13. See this discussed at length in Hindson, *Is the Antichrist Alive and Well?* (Eugene, OR: Harvest House, 1998).

14. Ice and Demy, *Truth About the Millennium*, p. 213.

CHAPTER 3

1. Cf. Gary DeMar, *Last Days Madness* (Brentwood, TN: Wolgemuth & Hyatt, 1991), pp. 10-11; Russell Chandler, *Doomsday* (Ann Arbor, MI: Servant Publications, 1993), p. 40.

2. Chandler, *Doomsday*, p. 39.

3. John Souter, "The Sky Is Falling," in *Future* (Wheaton, IL: Tyndale House, 1984), p. 6.

4. DeMar, *Last Days,* p. 11.

5. Chandler, *Doomsday,* pp. 47-48. Cf. also, Marvin Pate and Calvin Haines, *Doomsday Delusions* (Downers Grove, IL: InterVarsity Press, 1995), pp. 19-20.

6. See Edward E. Hindson, *Introduction to Puritan Theology* (Grand Rapids, MI: Baker, 1976), P.E. Hughes, *Theology of the English Reformers* (Grand Rapids, MI: Eerdmans, 1965).

7. This is examined at great length and detail in Paul Christianson, *Reformers and Babylon* (Toronto: University of Toronto, 1978); K.R. Firth, *The Apocalyptic Traditions in Reformation Britain* (Oxford: Oxford University, 1979); Hindson, *The Puritan's Use of Scripture in the Development of an Apocalyptical Hermeneutic* (Pretoria: University of South Africa, 1984); W. Haller, *"Foxe's Book of Martyrs" and the Elect Nation* (New York: Harper & Row, 1963); Christopher Hill, *Antichrist in Seventeenth-Century England* (London: Oxford University, 1971); Tai Liu, *Discord in Zion: The Puritan Divines and the Puritan Revolution 1640–1660* (The Hague: Martinus Nijhoff, 1973).

8. See S. Ozment, *The Age of Reform 1250–1550: An Intellectual and Religious History of Late Medieval and Reformation Europe* (New Haven: Yale University, 1980), pp. 103-15; M. Reeves, *The Influence of Prophecy in the Later Middle Ages: A Study of Joachimism* (Oxford: Clarendon, 1969).

9. John Wycliffe, *Select English Writings* (Oxford: Oxford University, 1929), pp. 66-74.

10. See details in Firth, *Apocalyptic Traditions in Reformation Britain,* pp. 11-15; J.M. Headley, *Luther's View of Church History* (New Haven: Yale University, 1963), pp. 141-46; M. Reeves, *Influence of Prophecy in the Later Middle Ages,* pp. 233-35.

11. John Calvin, *Commentary on Romans and Thessalonians,* trans. R. Mackenzie, in Calvin's commentaries, ed. Torrance & Torrance (Grand Rapids, MI: Eerdmans, 1959–1972), vol. 4, pp. 396-99; and *The First Epistle of John,* trans. T.H.L. Parker, vol. 3, p. 256.

12. John Bale, "The Image of Both Churches," in *Select Works of Bishop Bale* (London: Parker Society, 1948), and "A Comedy Concerning Three Laws," in J.S. Farmer, ed., *The Dramatic Writings of John Bale, Bishop of Ossory* (London: Early English Drama Society, 1907). Cf. also J. Harris, *John Bale: A Study in the Minor Literature of the Reformation* (Urbana: University of Illinois, 1940); H. McCusker, *John Bale: Dramatist and Antiquary* (Bryn Mawr: Haverford College, 1952); and Firth, *Apocalyptic Traditions,* pp. 32-68).

13. Walter Raleigh, *History of the World* in *The Works of Sir Walter Raleigh* (Oxford: Oxford University, 1829), Book 1, chap. 8, sec. 4, vol. 2, pp. 261-65; Book 5, chap. 6, sec. 12, vol. 1, pp. 898-900.

14. Hugh Broughton, *A Revelation of the Apocalypse* (Amsterdam: 1610), pp. 137-250. Cf. comments by Firth, *Apocalyptic Traditions,* pp. 152-63 and Christianson, *Reformers and Babylon,* pp. 107-11. The latter remarked of Broughton's date, "He could still be right!" (p. 109).

15. John Napier, *A Plaine Discovery of the Whole Revelation of St. John* (Edinburgh: 1593 and London: 1611). Cf. also R. Clouse, "John Napier and Apocalyptic Thought," *Sixteenth Century Journal,* V (1974), pp. 101-14.

16. His writings are collected in *The Works of Thomas Brightman* (London: 1644). Cf. also R. Clouse, "The Apocalyptic Interpretation of Thomas Brightman and Joseph Mede," *Bulletin of the Evangelical Theological Society,* XI (1968), pp. 181-93.

17. Joseph Mede, *The Key of the Revelation* (London: 1643). The Latin edition appeared in 1627. Cf. also his *Apostasy of the Latter Times* (London: 1642). On the significance of Mede's views, see Peter Toon, *Puritans, the Millennium and the Future of Israel* (London: James Clarke, 1970), pp. 42-56.

18. *A Glimpse of Zion's Glory* (London: 1641) and *A Sermon to the Fifth Monarch* (London: 1654). Cf. also Toon, *Puritans,* pp. 64-65 and Appendix I.

19. John Owen, "Righteous Zeal Encouraged by Divine Protection" (31 Jan. 1649), in *Works of John Owen* (London: W.H. Goold, 1850–1853), vol. 8, pp. 128ff.

20. See the excellent discussion in Charles Ryrie, *Dispensationalism Today* (Chicago: Moody, 1965), pp. 71-75.

21. See Clarence Bass, *Backgrounds to Dispensationalism* (Grand Rapids, MI: Eerdmans, 1960), pp. 64-99.

22. *The Collected Writings of J.N. Darby,* (London: Morrish, 1867), vol. 2, pp. 568-73.

23. This is the scheme generally followed in the *Scofield Reference Bible* (New York: Oxford University, 1909) and slightly modified in the *New Scofield Reference Bible* (1967).

24. For a thorough account of the history, beliefs, and practices of Mormons, Adventists, and Jehovah's Witnesses, see Anthony Hoekema, *The Four Major Cults* (Grand Rapids, MI: Zondervan, 1963).

25. See the excellent analysis of this by Stanley N. Gundry, "Hermeneutics or *Zeitgeist* as the Determining Factor in the History of Eschatologies?" *Journal of the Evangelical Theological Society,* 20:1 (1977), p. 50ff.

26. For an excellent discussion of what is happening in Europe today, see Grant Jeffrey, "The Rise of the European Super State," in *Prince of Darkness* (Toronto: Frontier Research Publications, 1994), pp. 112-24.

27. Daniel R. Mitchell, "Is the Rapture on Schedule?" *Fundamentalist Journal* (Oct. 1988), p. 66.

CHAPTER 4

1. John Walvoord, *Matthew: Thy Kingdom Come* (Chicago: Moody, 1974), p. 181. Cf. Also Edward E. Hindson, "Matthew," in *Parallel Bible Commentary,* ed. E. Hindson and W. Kroll (Nashville: Thomas Nelson, 1983), pp. 1946-52.

2. Cf. Homer Kent Jr., "Matthew," in *Wycliffe Bible Commentary* (Chicago: Moody, 1962), p. 85ff.

3. William S. LaSor, *The Truth About Armageddon* (Grand Rapids, MI: Baker, 1982), p. 15.

4. J.P. Lange, *Commentary on the Holy Scriptures: Matthew* (Grand Rapids, MI: Zondervan, n.d.), p. 428.

5. W.F. Arndt and F.W. Gingrich, *A Greek-English Lexicon of the New Testament* (Chicago: University of Chicago, 1957), p. 153.

6. R.C. Sproul, *The Last Days According to Jesus* (Grand Rapids, MI: Baker, 1998), pp. 49-68.

7. LaSor, *The Truth About Armageddon,* p. 122.

8. See Amos 5:18-20; Joel 1:15; 2:1,11,31; Isaiah 2:11-19; 13:6-9; 22:5; 34:8; Jeremiah 46:10; Zephaniah 1:7-8; Ezekiel 7:10, 13:5; 30:3; and Zechariah 14:1.

Chapter 5

1. For a detailed account, see Richard Lee and Ed Hindson, *Angels of Deceit* (Eugene, OR: Harvest House, 1993).

2. C.S. Lewis, *Mere Christianity* (New York: Macmillan, 1960), pp. 53-54.

3. Mary Baker Eddy, *Science and Health with Key to the Scriptures* (Boston: Trustees, 1925), p. 150.

4. Ibid., pp. vii-viii.

5. Hank Hanegraaff, *Christianity in Crisis* (Eugene, OR: Harvest House, 1993).

6. Elena Whiteside, *The Way: Living in Love* (New Knoxville, OH: American Christian Press, 1972), p. 178.

7. *The Way* magazine, September–October, 1974, p. 7.

8. Josh McDowell and Don Stewart, *Understanding the Cults* (San Bernardino, CA: Here's Life Publishers, 1986), p. 142.

9. Moses David, *Reorganization, Nationalization, Revolution!* (Rome: Children of God, 1970), DO #650.

10. See Caroll Stonner and Jo Anne Parke, *All God's Children* (Radnor, PA: Chilton Books, 1977), pp. 65ff. See also the compelling inside story by Berg's daughter, Deborah Davis (Linda Berg), *The Children of God* (Grand Rapids, MI: Zondervan, 1984).

11. Una McManus and John Cooper, *Dealing with Destructive Cults* (Grand Rapids, MI: Zondervan, 1984), pp.119-20.

12. Ibid., p. 118.

13. *You May Survive Armageddon into God's New World* (Brooklyn, NY: Watchtower Bible and Tract Society, 1955), p. 342. See also Anthony Hockeman, *The Four Major Cults* (Grand Rapids, MI: Eerdmans, 1984), pp. 307-12.

14. *Discourses of Brigham Young* (Salt Lake City: Deseret Book Co., 1954), p. 435.

15. Series of pamphlets, No. III., p. 8, quoted by Hoekema, *Four Major Cults,* p. 63.

16. Hoekema, *Four Major Cults,* pp. 139-40.

17. Eddy, *Science and Health,* pp. 456-57.

18. Ibid., p. 583.

19. *What Is Spiritualism?* Spiritualist Manual Revision of 1940, quoted by Walter R. Martin, *Kingdom of the Cults* (Minneapolis: Bethany Fellowship, 1965), p. 209.

20. Ibid., p. 210.

21. *Many Mansions,* p. 107, quoted by Martin, *Kingdom of the Cults,* p. 210.

22. Ibid., p. 250.

23. Ibid., p. 246.

24. Ibid., p. 312.

25. Sun Myung Moon, "Our Shame," *Master Speaks,* March 11, 1973, p. 3.

26. Moon, *The Way of the World,* p. 20, quoted by Josh McDowell and Don Stewart, *Understanding the Cults,* p. 134.

27. Cf. Ronald Enroth, et al., *A Guide to Cults & New Religions* (Downers Grove, IL: InterVarsity Press, 1983), pp. 104-05; and Martin, *Kingdom of the Cults,* pp. 87-101.

28. See Jehovah's Witness publications *Qualified to Be Ministers,* pp. 283-97, and *You May Survive Armageddon,* pp. 252ff. See also Hoekema, *Four Major Cults,* pp. 287-97.

29. Jack Sparks, *The Mind Benders* (Nashville: Thomas Nelson, 1977), p. 135.

30. "Zealot of God," *People* magazine, March 15, 1993, pp. 38-43.

31. "Radical Sheik," *Newsweek,* March 15, 1993, p. 32.

32. Una McManus and John Cooper, *Dealing with Destructive Cults* (Grand Rapids, MI: Zondervan, 1984), p. 117.

CHAPTER 6

1. Hobart Freeman, *An Introduction to the Old Testament Prophets* (Chicago: Moody Press, 1968), p. 126.

2. Leon Wood, *The Prophets of Israel* (Grand Rapids, MI: Baker, 1979), p. 67.

3. H.L. Ellison, *Men Spake from God* (Grand Rapids, MI: Eerdmans, 1952), p. 14.

4. R.B. Girdlestone, *Old Testament Theology* (London: Longmans, Green & Co., 1909), p. 120.

5. J.A. Alexander, *The Earlier Prophecies of Isaiah* (New York: Wiley & Putnam, 1846), p. 170.

6. Robert Culver, "Were the Old Testament Prophecies Really Prophetic?" in *Can I Trust My Bible?* (Chicago: Moody Press, 1963), pp. 99-101.

7. Willis Beecher, *The Prophets and the Promise* (New York: Crowell, 1905), p. 394.

8. Edward J. Young, *My Servants the Prophets* (Grand Rapids, MI: Eerdmans, 1952), p. 191.

9. Culver, p. 91. His excellent article should be consulted throughout pp. 91-116.

10. Ibid., p. 10.

11. John Phillips, *Only God Can Prophesy!* (Wheaton, IL: Harold Shaw, 1975), p. 11.

12. H.L. Ellison, *The Message of the Old Testament* (Palm Springs, CA: Ronald Haynes, 1981), p. 64.

CHAPTER 7

1. John Feinberg, "Arguing for the Rapture: Who Must Prove What and How?" paper presented to the Pre-Trib Research Center; quoted by Thomas Ice, in "Why the Rapture and the Second Coming are Distinct Events," *Pre-Trib Answers to Post-Trib Questions* (Aug.–Sept. 1994), p. 2.

2. Millard Erickson, *Christian Theology* (Grand Rapids, MI: Baker Book House, 1985), p. 1186.

3. Ice, "Why the Rapture and Second Coming are Distinct Events," in *Pre-Trib Answers to Post-Trib Questions (*Aug.–Sept. 1994), p. 2.

4. Ibid., p. 3.

5. Cf. Robert Gundry, *The Church and the Tribulation* (Grand Rapids, MI: Zondervan, 1973), pp. 85-86.

6. C.F. Hogg and W.E. Vine *The Epistles to the Thessalonians* (London: Exeter Press, 1929), p. 144.

7. Ibid., p. 242.

8. George Milligan, *St. Paul's Epistles to the Thessalonians* (Old Tappan, NY: Revell, 1908), vol. 2, p. 96. Cf. also A.T. Robertson, *Word Pictures in the New Testament* (Grand Rapids, MI: Baker, 1931 reprint), vol. IV, p. 47. He also notes that it refers to the rapture in 2 Thessalonians 2:1.

9. Cf. W.S. LaSor, *The Truth About Armageddon* (Grand Rapids, MI: Baker Book House, 1982), pp. 120-34; and G.E. Ladd, *The Blessed Hope* (Grand Rapids, MI: Eerdmans, 1956), pp. 71-104.

10. These may be found in an expanded version in Edward E. Hindson, *Final Signs* (Eugene, OR: Harvest House, 1996), pp. 66-73.

11. Dave Hunt, *Global Peace and the Rise of Antichrist* (Eugene, OR: Harvest House, 1990), p. 280.

12. Ibid., p. 283.

13. I.D.E. Thomas, *Golden Treasury of Puritan Quotations* (Chicago: Moody Press, 1975), p. 106.

CHAPTER 8

1. For a thorough exposition of these chapters in Revelation, see Edward E. Hindson, *Approaching Armageddon* (Eugene, OR: Harvest House, 1997), pp. 107-83.

2. Arthur Levine *When Dreams and Heroes Died* (San Francisco: Jossey-Bass, 1980).

3. John Phillips, *Only God Can Prophesy!* (Wheaton, IL: Harold Shaw, 1975), pp. 111-12.

4. Alfred Edersheim, *The Temple* (Grand Rapids, MI: Eerdmans, 1963), pp. 162-68.

5. Bruce Metzger, *Breaking the Code: Understanding the Book of Revelation* (Nashville: Abingdon Press, 1993), p. 63.

6. Phillips, *Only God Can Prophesy!* p. 113.

7. Leon Morris, *The Revelation of St. John* (Grand Rapids, MI: Eerdmans, 1969), p. 124.

8. John Walvoord, *The Revelation of Jesus Christ* (Chicago: Moody Press, 1966), p. 139.

9. Ibid., pp. 142-49.

10. Cf. Robert Thomas, *Revelation 1–7* and *Revelation 8–22: An Exegetical Commentary* (Chicago: Moody Press, 1992), on these sections of Revelation.

CHAPTER 9

1. Rene Pache, *The Return of Jesus Christ* (Chicago: Moody Press, 1955), p. 353.

2. Robert Gromacki, "Where is 'the Church' in Revelation 4-19?" in Thomas Ice and Timothy Demy, eds., *When the Trumpet Sounds* (Eugene, OR: Harvest House, 1995), p. 355.

3. G.R. Beasley-Murray, *The Book of Revelation* (London: Marshall, Morgan & Scott, 1978), p. 270.

4. Ibid., p. 271.

5. Ibid., pp. 273-74.

6. Bruce Metzger: *Breaking the Code:Understanding the Book of Revelation* (Nashville: Abingdon Press, 1993), p. 90.

7. J. Dwight Pentecost, *Things to Come* (Grand Rapids, MI: Zondervan, 1958), p. 226.

8. Metzger, *Breaking the Code,* p. 90.

9. A.W. Boehm, "Preface" to Johann Arndt's *True Christianity* (London: Brown & Downing, 1720), p. xxii.

CHAPTER 10

1. George Ladd, *Crucial Questions About the Kingdom of God* (Grand Rapids, MI: Eerdmans, 1952), p. 78.

2. Alva McClain, *The Greatness of the Kingdom* (Chicago: Moody Press, 1959), pp. 17, 41.

3. William S. LaSor, *The Truth About Armageddon* (Grand Rapids, MI: Baker, 1982), pp. 160-61.

4. John Walvoord, *Prophecy* (Nashville: Thomas Nelson, 1993), p. 139.

5. Robert Mounce, *The Book of Revelation* (Grand Rapids, MI: Eerdmans, 1977), p. 353.

6. Walvoord, *The Revelation of Jesus Christ* (Chicago: Moody Press, 1966), p. 292.

7. Thomas Ice and Timothy Demy, *The Millennium* (Eugene, OR: Harvest House, 1996), p. 8. Cf. also Mal Couch and Gordon Johnston, "Millennium," in Mal Couch, ed., *Dictionary of Premillennial Theology* (Grand Rapids, MI: Kregel, 1996), pp. 167-72.

8. Harold Hoehner, "Evidence from Revelation," in D. Campbell and J. Townsend, eds., *A Case for Premillennialism* (Chicago: Moody Press, 1992), pp. 249-50.

9. T.F. Torrance, "The Israel of God," *Interpretation* (July 1956), p. 317. Quoted by McClain, p. 463.

10. G.R. Beasley-Murray, *The Book of Revelation* (London: Marshall, Morgan & Scott, 1978), p. 287.

11. Rene Pache, *The Return of Christ* (Chicago: Moody Press, 1955), p. 381.

12. Beasley-Murray, *The Book of Revelation*, pp. 292-93.

13. Robert Thomas, *Revelation 8–22: An Exegetical Commentary* (Chicago: Moody Press, 1995), p. 429.

14. Ibid.

CHAPTER 11

1. Wilbur Smith, *The Biblical Doctrine of Heaven* (Chicago: Moody Press, 1968), p. 239.

2. Robert Thomas, *Revelation 8–22: An Exegetical Commentary* (Chicago: Moody Press, 1995), p. 442.

3. A.T. Robertson, *Word Pictures in the New Testament* (Grand Rapids, MI: Eerdmans, 1933), Vol. VI, p. 467.

4. G.R. Beasley-Murray, *The Book of Revelation* (London: Marshall, Morgan & Scott, 1978), p. 315.

5. John MacArthur, *The Glory of Heaven* (Wheaton, IL: Crossway Books, 1996), p. 86.

6. John Walvoord, *The Revelation of Jesus Christ* (Chicago: Moody Press, 1966), p. 330.

CHAPTER 12

1. Erwin Lutzer, *Where Do We Go from Here?* (Chicago: Moody Press, 1993), pp. 25-48.

2. Bill Hybles, *Becoming a Contagious Christian* (Grand Rapids, MI: Zondervan, 1994), pp. 43, 59.

3. Dave Hunt, *Whatever Happened to Heaven?* (Eugene, OR: Harvest House, 1988), p. 7.

4. Joseph Stowell, "Set Your Mind on Heaven," in *10 Reasons Why Jesus Is Coming Soon* (Sisters, OR: Multnomah Books, 1998), p. 235 ff.

5. C.S. Lewis, *Mere Christianity* (New York: Macmillan, 1943), p. 118.

6. Quoted by Lutzer, p. 46.

7. Quoted by Lutzer, p. 47.

8. Bailey Smith, *Taking Back the Gospel* (Eugene, OR: Harvest House, 1999), p. 8.

CHAPTER 13

1. John Walvoord, *Matthew: Thy Kingdom Come* (Chicago: Moody Press, 1974), p. 197.

2. Joseph Stowell, "Set Your Mind on Heaven," in *10 Reasons Why Jesus Is Coming Soon* (Sisters, OR: Multnomah Books, 1998), p. 252.

Bibliography

Dobson, Ed. *The End.* Grand Rapids: Zondervan, 1998.

Frazier, Gary. *Seven Signs of the Second Coming of Christ.* Arlington, TX: Discovery Ministries, 1998.

Hindson, Ed. *Final Signs.* Eugene, OR: Harvest House, 1996.

———. *Approaching Armageddon.* Eugene, OR: Harvest House, 1997.

———. *Is the Antichrist Alive and Well?* Eugene, OR: Harvest House, 1998.

Hoyt, Herman. *The End Times.* Chicago: Moody Press, 1969.

Hunt, Dave. *Global Peace and the Rise of the Antichrist.* Eugene, OR: Harvest House, 1990.

Ice, Thomas and Timothy Demy. *When the Trumpet Sounds.* Eugene, OR: Harvest House, 1995.

Jeffrey, Grant. *Armageddon: Appointment with Destiny.* New York: Bantam Books, 1991.

Jeremiah, David. *Escape the Coming Night.* Dallas: Word Publishing, 1990.

LaHaye, Tim. *Understanding the Last Days.* Eugene, OR: Harvest House, 1998.

Lalonde, Peter. *One World Under AntiChrist.* Eugene, OR: Harvest House, 1991.

Lee, Richard and Ed Hindson. *Angels of Deceit.* Eugene, OR: Harvest House, 1993.

Lindsey, Hal. *The Late Great Planet Earth.* Grand Rapids: Zondervan, 1970.

Pentecost, Dwight. *Things to Come.* Grand Rapids: Zondervan, 1975.

Reagan, David. *The Master Plan.* Eugene, OR: Harvest House, 1993.

Ryrie, Charles. *What You Should Know About the Rapture.* Chicago: Moody Press, 1981.

Showers, Renald. *Maranatha: Our Lord Come!* Bellmawr, NJ: Friends of Israel, 1995.

Stanton, Gerald. *Kept from the Hour.* Miami: Schoettle Publishing, 1991.

Walvoord, John. *Armageddon, Oil and the Middle East Crisis.* Grand Rapids, MI: Zondervan, 1990.

———. *Major Bible Prophecies.* New York: Harper Collins, 1991.

Willmington, Harold. *The King Is Coming.* Wheaton, IL: Tyndale House, 1991.

About the Author

Dr. Ed Hindson is the assistant pastor of the 9,000-member Rehoboth Baptist Church in Atlanta, Georgia. He also serves as dean of the Institute of Biblical Studies at Liberty University in Virginia. In addition, Dr. Hindson serves on the executive board of the Pre-Trib Research Center in Washington, D.C., and is a Life Fellow of the International Biographical Association in Cambridge, England. He holds degrees from several institutions, including: B.A., William Tyndale College; M.A., Trinity Evangelical Divinity School; Th.M., Grace Theological Seminary; Th.D., Trinity Graduate School; D.Min., Westminster Theological Seminary; and D.Phil., University of South Africa. He has also done graduate work at Acadia University in Nova Scotia, Canada.

Dr. Hindson has lectured at numerous schools, including Oxford University and the Harvard Divinity School. He has authored twenty books, including *Final Signs* (1996), *Approaching Armageddon* (1997) and *Is the Antichrist Alive and Well?* (1998), all published by Harvest House. He has also contributed to numerous publications including *The Premillennial Dictionary of Theology* (Kregel).

Dr. Hindson has been named in *Who's Who in Religion, Outstanding Personalities of America,* and the *International Who's Who of Intellectuals.* He combines a balance of biblical scholarship with the heart of a pastor and the tongue of a communicator. His style is both provocative and practical. He has taught more than 30,000 students in the past thirty years and ministered to thousands more through radio and television.